the four elements
of change

HEATHER ASH

Foreword by Vicki Noble

Council Oak Books, LLC

San Francisco / Tulsa

Council Oak Books
Tulsa, OK

Published 2004
Printed in Canada

10 09 08 07 06 05 04   1 2 3 4 5

ISBN 1-57178-123-4

Portions of the present work appeared in a slightly different version in *The Four Elements of Change: Tools for Living a Centered Life,* ©2003 by Heather MacKenzie-Gaudet.

contents

acknowledgments

My gratitude goes out to the many people who have supported me over the years.

First, to my parents, Jerry and Maggie Gaudet, and to my sister, Christy, who held such a strong container for a childhood of adventure and travel. I love you.

Many blessings to my teachers and guides over the years: Vicki Noble, Cerridwen Fallingstar, Peggy Dylan, and my dearest don Miguel Ruiz. Deep gratitude also to my teaching partner and mentor Gini Gentry for shining your light so brightly and helping me find my own path.

To my first coven sisters, Autumn Labbe-Renault, Isis Ward, Saurin Shine, Sana Banks, Heather Wahanik, Aimee Carroll: Yes!

To my dear Toltec family for being such beautiful mirrors, especially Ted and Peggy Raess, Laurence Andrews, Stephen Siegel, Chuck and Tink Cowgill, Francis Puerto-Hayhurst, Allan Hardman, Jules J. Frank, Ed Fox, Siri Gian Singh Khalsa, Stephen Collector, Rita Rivera, Gary van Warmerdam, Leo van Warmerdam, Barbara Simon, Niki Orrietas, Roberto Paez, Gae

Buckley, Sheri Rosenthal, and Stephanie Bureau, Lee McCormick and all the family of The Ranch and Spirit Recovery, among many others: *Que tu sol sea brillante.*

To the SpiritWeavers teachers, and to the community and the board of directors of the Toltec Center of Creative Intent, including but not limited to Jordan King, Storm Florez, Alice Lancefield, Indigo Flores, Audrey Lehmann, Eleanor Mahood, Raven Smith, Michele Murphy, Hannah Hughes, Theresa Bucci, Revi Airborne, Kirsten "Sunshine" Hardenbrook, Leslee Morrison, Alice Ruby, Diane Adkins, Rachel Ohliger, Ruth Masterson, Kim Christensen, Dakini Kalhoff, Shkiba Samimi-Amri, and Miriam Jeannette Castañeda.

To all friends, past, present, and future, for being teachers and inspirations, especially Craig, Rowan, Kyra and Nash Labbe-Renault, Jesikah Maria Ross, Thom Sterling, Poppy Davis, the Normal family and WEF. Many, many blessings to Kevin Braheny Fortune for your love and support during the first draft of this book.

To my two business and life mentors, Janet Mills and Jo Miller, for their faith and love, and for encouraging me to follow my vision.

To the great team at Council Oak Books: Paulette Millichap, Ja-lene Clark, Laura Woods, Sally Dennison, Vanessa Perez. Your enthusiasm and excitement about this project sustained and motivated me to share my best.

Special thanks to Jorge Luis Delgado and the wonderful staff of Taypikala Hotel on Lake Titicaca in Peru for creating a nurturing space for me to dream and write.

And overflowing gratitude to my business partner, life partner, husband, lover, and all around playmate Raven Smith. Dearest one, thank you for sharing your light with me and inspiring me in so many ways. I am truly blessed.

May these words help all beings
balance mind, spirit, emotions, and body,
and return to their true divine center.

foreword
by Vicki Noble

The four elements have been recognized and honored for many thousands of years, as can be seen in art and archaeological artifacts from the ancient civilizations of the Americas, Old Europe, Africa, the Middle East, China, India and Tibet. There are probably as many ways of conceptualizing the four elements as there are different peoples around the world, and yet the basic structure remains fundamentally the same. Calling in the water, wind, earth and fire grounds us in physical reality while opening us in a sacred way.

Regardless of origin, pictorial representations from different cultures share a structure consisting of four sacred or holy beings arranged in the cardinal directions around a central figure or symbol. Some of the earliest Navaho sand paintings on record bear an uncanny resemblance, for example, to ceramic plates excavated from sites on the other side of the world in Iran that are thousands of years old. Similarly, a Navaho sand painting created at a museum in the Southwest in the 1950s depicts "Whirling Rainbow People from

Windway" not at all unlike the Tibetan Buddhist concept of "Dakinis" (female beings who fly through space) who, when invoked from the four cardinal directions and the center, come whirling in like vases.

In the European tradition, the East represents the element of air and the dawning of consciousness; the Southern lands of the equator suggest fire and noonday passion; the Western ocean points to water and the nostalgic feelings aroused by the sunset; while in the North we see the earth element in the cold regions of the Arctic at midwinter. When Karen Vogel and I made the Motherpeace tarot cards in the late 1970s, we were working with this exact system. Modern shamans "call in" the directions in rituals celebrated on holidays marking the days of the seasonal calendar that correspond to the same cardinal directions and their intermediary cross-quarter days.

The special gift of this book is the unique synthesis that Heather Ash is able to make by blending everything she has learned about the elements over the course of her life as a Western spiritual seeker. Speaking directly to her peers, Heather Ash translates the ancient system into a tool for these faster, more secular times in which we live, offering modern people a way of transforming their lives and releasing the obstacles that block their way to serenity and well-being. She offers advice and encouragement every step of the way, sharing stories from her own experience and observations from her work with students over the years, grounding the teachings in the day-to-day struggles of real people in today's world.

Heather's approach offers an accessible path in these urgent times. The simplicity of it makes it possible for people to use the method in spite of being overwhelmed with other obligations. Imagine if each of us could find his or her way back to the center of our own being with the help of the healing power of elements, we might generate peace and love on this planet! May it be so for every reader of this book, and may the principles and practices of the four directions be alive and well in our lives once more.

Blessed Be.

What is life? It is a flash of a firefly in the night. It is the breath of a buffalo in the wintertime. It is the little shadow which runs across the grass and loses itself in the sunset.

Crowfoot

INTRODUCTION

the four elements

The elements of air, fire, water, and earth are the foundation of life. From the air we breathe to the earth beneath our feet, from the water we drink to the heat of the sun, each of the elements is vital to our very existence. Without just one of these elements, all life on the planet would cease to exist.

The four elements are powerful guides for how to live in alignment with nature and our own essence. Every breath of air brings more spaciousness into our being. Fire invites us to expand into more vibrancy. We learn to become fluid like water. The earth reminds us to live fully in our bodies. Each element is a tool for becoming more present and vital.

When we align with the four elements, we tap into the wisdom of life itself.

Native peoples around the world have always honored the four elements as ever-present allies. From Native American traditions to the roots of Buddhism, from African ritual to European shamanic wisdom, the elements of air, fire, water, and earth weave into the core of every spiritual tradition. By following the wisdom passed down through the lineages of native peoples, we can use the elements as potent tools for bringing balance and magical purpose back into our lives.

The elements were used as guideposts of transformation for the Toltecs in Teotihuacan, Mexico. The huge pyramid complex of Teotihuacan was designed as a physical reflection of the inner journey to connect with the Divine. This powerful place of initiation continues to draw those who are ready to release their fear-based attachments and reclaim their authentic power. People begin the process at the plaza of earth where they symbolically bury their physical bodies and move through the plaza of water to release the emotional body, the plaza of air to free the mental bodies, and the plaza of fire to ignite the spiritual body. This process purifies and aligns the self to its essence.

maɡɪcaL Lɪvɪnɢ

Many of us in modern times fall short of living our fullest potential. Our struggle to consciously manifest what we desire (whether this is enlightenment or doing better in school) is due to our being out of balance internally. We rely on our minds (air), but ignore our emotional bodies (water). We focus on our physical bodies (earth), and forget about our spiritual essence (fire). Because of this imbalance, a sense of deep satisfaction and joyful participation in our own destiny is missing.

To live magically means to live in pure, open awareness of all possibilities while being able to focus to create specific change. Magical living allows us to focus our deepest purpose to systematically create positive change in all aspects of life.

Each of us has the potential to be a master of balanced change. When we step into our authentic self, we connect to our highest source of inspiration and potential. We create our soul's desire on the physical plane by following our heart's impulses instead of our unconscious conditioning. Our lives transform from struggle and survival to joy and clear purpose.

BaLaNcɪNɢ tHe seLf

As we learn to live magically, we begin to embody the balance of mind, spirit, emotions, and body. This is not a static state of being, but a dynamic, a dance. We must consciously bring the four parts of self into awareness to be examined and integrated.

Each of us has a tendency to rely on one part of our self and dismiss the others. For example, in the Western world we place great emphasis on the power of the mind, and minimize the wisdom of the emotions and intuition. Many of today's main religions create a split between the physical body and the spiritual being. Any kind of schism between the four parts of self creates conflict within the self. This internal chaos causes us to lose the energy we need to create positive change in our lives.

We can bring ourselves back to balance by using the four elements as reflections of the different aspects of ourselves. Just as one of the elements is not more or less important than any other, no one part of ourselves is more or less important. By keeping the four elements in our awareness on a daily basis, we set into motion our internal healing and integration. This is where the magic begins. This allows us to access the immense internal energy that is vital for change.

Living within the Cycles

Change is not linear, but a process of inspiration, fruition, deepening, death and rebirth. The four main markers of the year, spring equinox (air), summer solstice (fire), fall equinox (water), and winter solstice (earth), reflect how change actually occurs in nature and in humans.

In ancient times, individuals and communities would share in the cyclical changes of nature by coming together to celebrate the equinoxes and solstices. Every part of the cycle, from the recent deaths to the new births, was honored. Coming together in community gave every individual a stable marker to see what had changed for them internally since the last gathering. This allowed them to "feel into" those places where they wanted to put their energy in the coming months.

In modern times, we are becoming isolated from the cyclical nature of change. Electric lights, fixed work hours, and linear thinking all separate us from the natural ebb and flow of the natural world. Our ability to communicate instantaneously with each other via email and cell phones is programming us to expect transformation to happen this instant. We then apply this pressure to our own internal change process. The result is frustration, self-judgement, and confusion. When we align with the seasons of nature and the four elements the result is flow, faith, and patience.

Living in harmony: the four seasons of change

air: In the spring, new life is beginning to sprout. The seedling is poking its head through the soil, eager for the sun to help it grow.

All change begins with a seed thought, a focus. Everything humans have created, from tires to stories, began with a thought, an inspiration. We have many thoughts sprouting constantly. Spring reminds us that the energy of germination is so powerful, anything will grow. We must have clear vision to perceive which thoughts are based from our truth and which arise from our fears.

fire: Summer is the season of blossoming and tremendous energy. The days are long and the sun is at its firey fullest. This is a time of rapid expansion.

If we want to keep our seedling of change alive, we need to give it energy, life force, and to clear out what does not support its growth. Any thoughts or inspirations need to be energized. This is a time for action. One vital need now is for good weeding, to give the seedling a change to prosper. In our own process of manifestation, there will come a season when negative beliefs or thoughts spring up to overshadow our focus. We have to root them out.

water: Fall is a time of transition, when the leaves begin to fall and the earth begins to slow down. The rains come and we turn inward. Fall is a time of reflection and harvest.

Once we have clarified our vision and cleaned away anything that saps its energy, we move into a time of deepening. We have the opportunity to reflect on our initial intent and either energize it or release it. Fall reminds us to soften and open to the changes that are happening. Just as the trees do not clutch onto their leaves for fear of being exposed, we learn to open our hands and surrender to change. This is a time for harvesting the fruit of our intent, which sometimes does not look like what we have been expecting.

earth: Winter is a time of rest, and of death and rebirth. The earth is dormant and we move into the longest night of the year.

In the cycles of life, rest and death are a vital part of change. In winter, everything slows down. Our initial spring seed either dies back each year and nourishes the soil, or goes into a resting period. When we are manifesting intent we always need time to rest and reflect. Perhaps we need to accept the death of outdated beliefs, relationships, ways of perceiving ourselves. This period of rest helps us see what we must let go of in order to move on. This is a time for nourishing ourselves in silence and reflecting on the changes and growth we have made. Winter teaches us to pull inward and offer our gifts from the most essential nature of who we are.

As we reflect we can choose to release our initial intent and plant the seed of a new purpose, or re-energize our original intent, making it stronger and more focused for the next cycle. In this time of silence it may appear nothing is happening. But deep within the earth a new seed has been planted. It is gathering and storing energy, nourishing itself, for the coming burst of energy to sprout in the Spring.

The solstices and equinoxes mark a time of transition between seasons. The equinoxes mark when earth and sun are in perfect balance; day and night are the same length. Solstices mark the longest day or night of the year. But while a shift in the cycles of the sun in the earth occurs at each of these quarter days, these concrete changes are not noticed right away. After the winter solstice—the longest night of the year—there is more light than the day before. But we do not wake up on December 22 or 23 and say, "Hey, look, there is more light today! The sun is returning!" It is still really dark. A change has occurred, but the change has not become manifest yet.

Change follows this pattern in our lives as well. We might make a big shift in our lives internally, but we do not see the manifestation of this change for months or even years.

Change happens below the surface, before there is any visible progress. There is a season to rest and nourish ourselves, and there is a season take action.

These cycles of activity and rest, new growth and harvest mirror the process of manifesting any desire. We need to honor all parts of the cycle of change, internally and externally, to become the magicians of our life.

REBUILDING OUR 'HOUSE'

Our being is like a house, a tangible manifestation of the life force. Following the wisdom of native peoples, we can use the four elements as cornerstones to rebuild our "house" based on our authentic self. By using the four elements to balance the four parts of self and to align with the seasons, we gain the extra energy necessary to remodel our house in any manner we choose.

Remodeling begins by delving into the old structure. Our house, or our self, is something we created unconsciously and that no longers serves us. But which walls need to come down and what will anchor us during the renovation? The four elements can give us that anchor, if we learn to use them. They can empower us to rebuild our lives on a strong, magical foundation. From this new base, any change we choose to set into motion will become our reality.

*In oneself lies the whole world and if you
know how to look and learn, the door is there
and the key is in your hand. Nobody on earth
can give you either the key or the door to
open, except yourself.*

                              J. Krishnamarti

*May your walls know joy; May every room
hold laughter and every window open
to great possibility.*

                    Maryanne Radmacher-Hershey, 1995

tHIS oLD HOUSe

If you imagined yourself as a house, with your mind, spirit, emotions, and body as the four corners of your foundation, would your base be stable and supportive? Would each of the rooms in your house be decorated exactly like you wanted? Would your closets be clean? Would there be space and light and peace throughout?

Or would your internal house be in need of a good cleaning and remodeling?

Actually, we have been building the house of our self since childhood, often based on other people's designs. If you had all the resources necessary to remodel your life, how would you choose differently? What walls would you tear down? How would you want your house to feel?

Although remodeling oneself can be exhilarating, it is also disruptive. Throughout this book, we will learn how to call on the four elements to be our scaffolding, a safe container for change.

No matter how severe or minor the changes you want to make in your life, the Four Elements of Change will support you in making positive, concrete shifts in the actual structure of your being. Remodeling takes tools and skill, and this book will guide you step by step in gaining the awareness, energy, and action to create the life you have always wanted to live.

By creating more space and awareness in your life, you will be able to dissolve limiting beliefs and move past inner obstacles. You will learn to reclaim lost or stagnant energy, step fully into your power, and feel supported and vitalized by life.

These practices apply to all aspects of your life—from your work to your inner relationship with yourself and your outer relationships with friends, partners, and family. Change, no matter how eagerly awaited, is unsettling and involves a loss, a sacrifice of something. Moving is a loss of an old way of living. Aging is a loss of youth. From ending a relationship to getting sick to coming home from a great vacation, all transformation creates instability and takes a period of readjustment.

Using the four elements, you will find a compassionate structure to guide you and provide you with safe passage through the often choppy waters of personal change.

the structures that bind us

The resources in this book come from the most powerful and practical tools from a variety of spiritual traditions, combined with my own personal experience. I was blessed to study shamanic healing with Vicki Noble, co-creator of the *MotherPeace Tarot* deck, and to study and teach with don Miguel Ruiz, author of *The Four Agreements*. My apprenticeship with don Miguel began in 1994, when I approached him to teach me about the tarot. At that time I did not know that my work with the Toltec community would irrevokably change my life. Six years later he urged me to "go out into the world and make the teachings your own."

During my apprenticeship with don Miguel I learned how we all have the capacity to shift our perception and increase our energy to create positive change in our lives. As young children we learn to behave in certain ways that often cause us to go against our very nature. By learning how to become aware of and then release old structures, it is possible to reclaim our inner nature and live magically from our own truth.

Very young children are examples of pure, open exuberance for life. Before the age of two or three, children are carefree, wild, and curious. They are pure expression, wanting to test and taste everything. "Look, it's raining! Look, we got stuck in the mud!" When they are happy they laugh joyfully; when upset, they cry freely.

Before the introduction of adult concepts like good and bad, right and wrong, there is a pure flow of energy. But as the mind develops, a literal structure begins to be created within us, which limits our perception and causes a great deal of suffering.

Let's look at how these structures are created, and what the consequences are.

Pretend you are a young child playing rambunctiously with your brother in the house. You are laughing and running around gleefully. Suddenly you hear a loud crash, and you turn the corner to see that your brother has accidentally knocked over Mom's favorite vase, which shatters all over the floor.

You both freeze and look at each other, and then start laughing and playing again.

Your mom is on her way home, and has had a rotten day. She had a fight with her boss at work, she's been stuck in traffic, and she feels a headache coming on. All she wants is a little peace and quiet

When she walks in the door she hears her two children laughing and running around, and then sees her grandmother's favorite vase, the only thing her grandmother ever gave her, shattered all over the floor. What is her reaction?

Let's pretend that Mom has never yelled or gotten upset with her kids, but today she loses it. She starts yelling, "Who broke my vase?"

You and your brother come running into the front room to see what Mom is yelling at. You are both surprised when she screams at you about the vase, demanding to know who broke it.

Your brother looks at you and says, "She did it!"

You look at your brother and then your mother, stuttering, "I, I didn't..."

"You! Go to your room now!" Mom yells at you.

So perhaps feeling hurt for the first time, you go to your room and sit on your bed. Close your eyes for a minute and imagine you are that child, and you have just been falsely accused of something and punished. How do you feel?

Most likely, you feel hurt and betrayed. You might be angry at your brother for blaming you, and angry at your mother for believing him. You may feel scared that mom could get angry with you for no reason. There is a strong emotional reaction, a feeling in your body that fills you.

Can you imagine going to your room, sitting on your bed, and saying to yourself: "Wow, Mom was in a really bad mood! I hope she's okay! And Brother, he must have been really scared when he heard Mom yelling. He must have thought he was going to get in big trouble. Well, I will talk to both of them later and straighten it out." Can you imagine shrugging your shoulders and sitting down to color in your favorite coloring book? Highly unlikely...

If we were an internally focused and centered society, as children we might be able to say to ourselves, "I just got thrown in my room for something I didn't do; that feels bad," and then look inside ourselves for guidance. We might talk with ourselves and say, "Wow. That wasn't fair." But we would know that the anger wasn't directed towards us personally.

As children, we are energetically very sensitive, so we sponge up the agreements of the society around us. From a simple emotional response to a situation we then begin to make agreements about what it must mean that Brother did not get in trouble but we did. We do not feel safe, so we create agreements to try and keep this unsafe situation from happening again

And so, instead of knowing, "I'm a good person, and there has been confusion outside of me," you grab onto something that says, "I'm not a good person. Mom is upset with me. My brother's really mean. He must hate me." You start making agreements outside of yourself, as a way to try and understand the situation so you feel safe again.

What agreement might a child make from this situation? What agreement might you make? Close your eyes for a minute and just feel that. If at a really young age your mother had become really upset and angry with you because of something that somebody else had done, what agreement might you have made?

"Life's not fair."
"I'm bad, Mom doesn't love me."
"Nobody loves me."
"I don't trust anybody."
"It's not safe to play. I'll get in trouble."
"My brother is bad."

Instead of just experiencing and releasing an emotion about this scenario and moving on, the child makes an agreement, usually without even realizing that they are doing so. The problem is that this agreement gets locked in the body with the emotion, and will be played out in full over the years.

With these agreements the child begins to move away from her center. Let's say that the child's mind latches onto the agreement: "Mother loves Brother better." It might feel awful to the child to believe that her mother loves her brother better, but it creates a sense of control to know the "facts" about why she got in trouble.

Now to feel right she has to prove that this new agreement is true, so she knows that she is correct in her perception. So she goes back into the world with this new belief and finds proof to support it.

Even if Mother comes and apologizes and says she was sorry for getting so upset, the child's mind still needs to validate her new belief. So imagine that the family is now sitting at dinner, and Mother passes the peas to Brother first. "Aha!" says the girl to herself, "I knew it. Mom passed the peas to Brother first. She does love him better."

Later, if Mom passes the cake to her first she ignores it, still thinking about Mom passing her brother the peas.

And so the child begins to create a structure, a whole fortress of ideas and conditions. Mom likes Brother better, but I don't care anyway, I don't need anyone. Mom likes Brother better because I am bad. Mom likes Brother better because boys are more important than girls.

So this little being creates a structure in her mind that turns her away from her own center. From this one minor incident her vision is impaired and turned away from her own light. This is a relatively minor trauma, something she might not even remember when she grows up. But you can see what a huge impact it will have on her entire life. The seeds of this mental structure—I am bad, I don't need anyone, boys are more important than girls—will sprout and grow as long as she is not conscious of them. She will literally create a reality that will conform with this handful of unconscious childhood agreements.

As children, each of us took on beliefs and agreements that moved us away from our center. Many of these were passed on energetically from our parents, some we mimicked from what we saw around us, others we made up all on our own. These beliefs became a foundation for all of our future actions.

CREATING THE LIFE YOU WANT

Old agreements create a solid structure that we believe is who we really are, a belief system that traps us in the past. This structure causes us to react to present-day experiences from a very limited window of choice. The far-reaching ramifications of a simple childhood event can greatly weaken our foundation and affect all future experiences.

While working with many students to uncover their old structures, I learned that we grow to believe that the structure we have created is who we really are. We forget what it is like to be centered and confident in ourselves. Our sense of self becomes wrapped up in the strength of our structure. So when this structure is threatened in any way, fear arises, and our very stability is threatened.

Even when you consciously choose to change your structure, you may experience a great sense of fear and loss. The old agreements obviously no longer serve you. Your actions and behaviors clearly need to change. But when you begin to dismantle or rearrange the old structure, a force seems to stop or divert you.

Sometimes the closer you get to making a change, the less attractive it seems. You get distracted. You are thrown into chaos and even experience a sense of helpless terror. Or you find yourself getting very sleepy and dull.

Before I began working with the four elements consciously, I fearfully struggled with many of these issues. I learned that it is possible to greatly minimize the fears and distractions that arise for all of us as we dismantle our old structures. The four elements are the key. They offer a way to integrate transformation effectively as you transition between your old and new structures.

*We are the living links in a life force
that moves and plays around and
through us, binding the deepest soils
with the farthest stars.*

Alan Chadwick

DReam of tHe eLDeRS

my own healing journey from an unconscious to a conscious structure began nearly twenty years ago. Over the course of years of therapy, spiritual work, traveling, and teaching countless workshops, I noticed an interesting pattern in my life. My emotional breakthroughs or "healing—aha! moments—" were often followed by periods of depression, fear, and self-doubt. Not long after I broke through a fear, it would grab me around the ankles and haul me back to old behaviors. The structure of my old self was still alive and unwilling to change. I wondered if most people had similar experiences and if there was a way to facilitate a lasting change in structure while remaining centered.

In 1999, I dedicated over six months to intensely watching this reluctant-to-change part of myself and tracking it in my students. While much had changed for the better in my life, a few deeply rooted issues kept me out of balance. For example, even though I knew better, I clung to a relationship long after I would have been better off ending it. Even though my path was clearly taking me in another direction, I longed to go back to my old spiritual community, fearing I might miss out on something. Although my old life was shifting, I resisted the change. I continued to look outside myself for answers, and, to feel safe, I still tried to control other people's behavior.

I kept asking myself: "How do we step out of our limitations? Why do we keep going back to old behaviors, old relationships, and old ways of reacting? What is the key to lasting personal change?"

When we bring curiosity, patience, and openness to the questions in our lives, answers arrive in a multitude of forms. Mine came in a dream that crystallized years of work with many different teachers, healers, and spiritual traditions. The dream showed me a pathway to living a balanced life in the midst of great inner change. The pathway involved using the four elements to help me reclaim a sacred, possibility-centered life.

The dramatic shifts in my life and in the lives of many people I've worked with are the direct result of working with these four simple actions based on the four elements that accelerate and support deep, lasting change. These Four Elements of Change reflect a synthesis of the most powerful tools from many spiritual traditions, including European shamanism, Toltec wisdom, and Buddhism.

The Four Elements of Change form a synthesis, a flower grown from the soil of much direct experience, guidance, and experimentation. They reflect an integration of the most direct and practical spiritual and healing practices I have found, and provide a structure designed to create a container for rapid growth. I feel blessed to share them with you.

Below is the vision the elders shared with me in the dreamtime. The insights from this dream form the core of The Four Elements of Change.

the DReam of the eLDeRS

In a vast, soft green meadow we stand as a circle of beings embraced by a wide, violet-blue sky.

"At any moment, each human has the capacity to merge fully and completely into his or her center," one of the elders in the circle says.

"This takes a tremendous amount of focus, for it means stepping through your limiting structures," another says, looking directly into my eyes. "As individuals and in community, humans are at the cusp of a great change. The four elements of air, fire, water, and earth will guide people to embody their authentic selves."

A woman steps forward and leads me to a circle of stones. "Feel the tremendous love and peace that arises from living out of your true center," she says, inviting me to step inside and sit in the center of the circle. "Honor each element—air, fire, water, and earth—and it will share its wisdom with you."

As I sit on the warm earth, I offer a prayer to welcome the elements to teach me. I suddenly feel a presence in front of me, and open my eyes to see a woman dressed in soft yellows and golds. As she changes into a golden eagle and soars above my head, I know she is the representation of the element of air. She flies lower and lands on my shoulder, and I discover I can see through her eyes. I feel great peace, and a vastness of vision enlarges all my senses.

"Air represents your mind," she whispers, and I feel a shift within me that allows me to witness clear mind. Through the bird's eyes, the mind is a place of vision. It rests quietly, witnessing all that occurs. As she flaps her wings, the clarity dissolves and I see the mind out of balance. Everything becomes cluttered and loud. Voices compete for attention. The mind judges everything it sees, including itself. Clear vision is replaced by confusion. I feel fearful and alone.

"The gift of air is clear perception," I hear, and suddenly I can witness my mind without being drowned by its fears. "See with the eyes of the eagle. Align your mind with your center. Let the mind be supported by all of your being."

As she dissolves, I allow her words to touch my core. A few moments later I feel another being enter the circle. I turn to my right and find myself facing a huge, fiery panther.

"The gift of fire is cleansing," the panther says, arching its back. "Fire represents your spirit, your energetic body." As the panther stretches out a paw and softly brushes my hand, my body lights up with tendrils of energetic fire. I can see the places where my energy burns clearly and the places where an

inner structure blocks the flow of energy. My body tingles as energy rushes through and around it.

"*Use the fire to clean what does not serve you,*" *the panther says, taking a blocked part of my energy and feeding it to the fire. "Let your spirit shine brightly and align with your center." As the panther becomes a pure flame, I continue to watch my blocked energy burn away.*

Another being emerges in the circle to my right. A man made of water greets me. Inside of him I can see many forms of water: rain, tears, waterfalls, rivers, the ocean, the lightest mist. "Water represents your emotional body," he says, as simultaneously every emotion flows through him. "The gift of water is openness."

Within my body, I feel every place that has ever been closed suddenly open. I become pure flow, pure emotion. There is no difference between grief and joy. I feel enormous space in my body, and water flows around my structure, creating openings and fissures.

"*When you open, great change occurs. Open and find balance." The water man becomes a raging river, a gentle stream, and then a clear bowl of pure crystal water. As I drink from the bowl, pure emotion touches my center.*

I now turn to face the last element, that of earth. A snake appears and leads me down a hole, deep into the soil. "It is from here that you nourish the seed of your true self," the snake whispers. "I represent earth and the strength of the physical body. The gift of earth is nourishment."

As the snake speaks, I become a tree with roots deep in the earth. I feel in my body what nourishes me and what poisons me; what in my world is food, and what is toxic. "You instinctually know what feeds your center, and what feeds your structure. Choose wisely," *the snake says.*

As I transform from the tree into my human body, I feel a deep sense of wonder. I can sense all four elements illuminating my own center. They create a new structure that surrounds and holds me. I no longer feel alone or confused.

Once again, I am standing in the circle with the elders in the meadow. They speak to me of the journey of change: "To become the butterfly, a caterpillar needs a cocoon to create stability while massive changes occur. You can use the four elements as your cocoon, as your new home, while you dismantle the old."

"Use the Four Elements of Change as a map back to your true self, which is neither young nor old, but eternal," *one of the elders continues, opening his arms wide.* "Come into balance with the four elements of life. Each element represents a part of your being. When you bring the four elements into harmony, you will be in alignment with your center."

"Use these elements to support you while you dismantle the structure that keeps you trapped in fear," *another elder said, stepping forward to take my hands in hers.* "Then spread this message. Let the power of your new knowing emanate like warm rays of light to help others find their* centers. *We can only make great change in the world when we are centered within ourselves."*

The elders bless me and slowly dissolve. I stand alone in the meadow, embodying the qualities of air, fire, water, and earth. Taking a calm, full breath, I gaze at the vastness of sky and smile.

the four elements of change

The dream of the elders illustrates how the elements of air, fire, water, and earth are the building blocks of life. As you recreate yourself, these four elements become the building blocks of a new foundation. Each element represents a part of your being. When you integrate all four elements, you balance all parts of yourself and naturally live from your center.

Each of the elements has a complementary action—an art—for you to learn. We begin with air, but working with the four elements is not a linear process. The elements and their actions blend and support one another to create container for change.

AIR REPRESENTS THE MENTAL BODY. THE ACTION OF AIR IS CLEAR SEEING. The first element of change focuses on the art of clear perception. The journey to center is greatly speeded by a compassionate and supportive mind. Since we have spent so much time in negative thinking, the mind is probably one of the most difficult parts to change. With patience and practice and a conscious shift in attitude, moving from fearful mind to clear mind is possible.

FIRE REPRESENTS THE ENERGETIC BODY. THE ACTION OF FIRE IS CLEANING. Fire represents our spirit and the energetic aspect of our being. The second element in our circle, fire, teaches us about the wisdom of cleaning. The fire element is about action. After we witness through the eyes of air, we move into cleaning out what is no longer true. Cleaning is not something you do just once in your life, and then it's over. Action, just like learning to walk, is about repetition and practice.

WATER REPRESENTS THE EMOTIONAL BODY. THE ACTION OF WATER IS OPENING. The gift of water is learning to open ourselves to all things. It is easy to stay open to things we like or that feel good, and more difficult to stay open to things we dislike or that feel bad. To open means accepting all that life brings while simultaneously choosing to act for positive change. Opening is not a passive, discouraged acceptance of your inner world or outer reality. It is a courageous internal movement of trust into the new life that is unfolding.

EARTH REPRESENTS THE PHYSICAL BODY. THE ACTION OF EARTH IS NOURISHING. The final element in our circle is earth. Earth represents the physical body, and the need to nourish ourselves from the inside out. Opening allows us to delve into and clean the darker aspects of our being; the earth's nourishing aspects feed our center so it radiates vibrant health.

Read each of the four element chapters, and then choose the corresponding practice exercises that feel most relevant to you. These exercises will help you integrate the qualities of each element into your daily life. The final chapter explores how, once we embody the four elements, we prepare ourselves to step beyond our structure completely and into the fifth element, our essence.

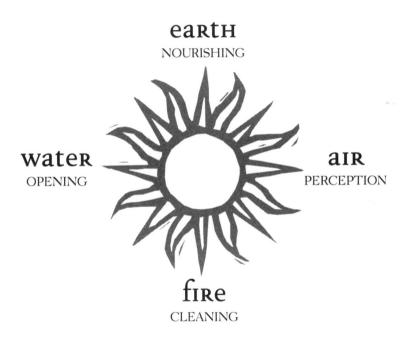

earth
NOURISHING

water
OPENING

air
PERCEPTION

fire
CLEANING

An arrow may fly through the air and leave no trace; but an ill thought leaves a trail like a serpent.

Mackay

When the doors of perception are cleansed, man will see things as they truly are, infinite.

William Blake (1757 - 1827)

AIR

the art of clear perception

modern society highly values the mind, often to the exclusion of the other aspects of self: spiritual, emotional, and physical. When the mind is out of balance with the rest of our being, fear results. Instead of going within to tap into the resources of spirit, emotions, and body, the mind grasps at external validation, substances, and people to feel stable and supported. Whatever we find outside of ourselves only brings a temporary sense of security, since it may be taken away at any time. The result of looking outside of ourselves for support is a worried mind.

This misuse of the mind results in us moving further and further away from our true center.

The first element of change focuses on the art of clear perception. The journey to center is greatly speeded by a compassionate and supportive mind. But changing the workings of the mind is not easy. Most of us have spent much time in negative thinking. It will require patience and practice and a conscious shift in attitude, but moving from fearful mind to clear mind is possible.

The various media reflect and nourish the fear and scarcity aspects of our minds and cloud our vision. They reflect how our culture reinforces looking outside ourselves for a sense of inner balance. When was the last time you saw an ad that read: "You are perfect exactly as you are. Would you like to buy our shampoo?" Most advertising is based on the premise of lack: "If you drink our beer, you will have the charisma you have always wanted" or "This car will give you the prestige and recognition you are looking for." The message over and over is: "You are not enough as you are, but if you just buy this gizmo, everything will be okay."

The news media also give us insight into why our minds love to worry. In the newspapers and on television news we are repetitively shown examples of war, murder, poverty, and instability in the world. The truth is, millions of different things are happening simultaneously around the world. Can you imagine picking up a major newspaper with a top headline reading "Woman Reaches Enlightenment, Full Story on Page 2"? Imagine how the different the world could be if we gave as much emphasis to spiritual development and joyous events in the media as we currently give to fear-based events.

The mind needs to come back in balance with all aspects of your being, particularly when it is tending to weave together exaggerated scenarios of scarcity and danger. I call this unbalanced state disaster mind. Also known as worst case scenario and negative mind, disaster mind is constantly scanning for what could go wrong. It thrives on judgment, comparison, fear, and scarcity. It lives in the past and the future, and is never settled in the present moment.

DISASTER MIND IN ACTION

Eight years ago I experienced the incredible strength of disaster mind when I chose to be in silence for forty days. This extended silence gave me the gap I needed to see the workings of my mind. During this time I saw my disaster mind in action, and I learned how to create the space to witness rather than believe everything my mind told me.

My intent for going into silence was to connect more deeply with my center. I wanted to give myself time off from interacting verbally and focus on my own inner sense of peace. The first few days of silence were wonderful. But silence and I had a short honeymoon. The next two weeks were perfect hell. Perfect, because what arose was exactly what I needed to see. Hell, because of the immense drama and judgment that was present in my mind much of the time.

When I first began my silence, I lived in a tiny cabin with no electricity, forty-five minutes out of town. The road to work was winding and steep, along a river ravine.

As I drove to town one morning, I was startled by the loudness of my mind. "You are late for work!" it screamed at me. "You are going to get fired!" Then my mind created a whole inner movie for me to watch: getting fired, losing my house, losing all my friends, and ending up destitute.

When that vision ran to the bitter end, another one started. "You are going too fast; you are going to go over the edge of the road!" I envisioned myself running through the guardrail and plunging over the edge to the river below. I saw myself dying or, even worse, trapped in the car, still alive but badly mangled, with no one to help me.

"What is my mind doing?" I asked myself. I felt split in two: One part of me was watching a completely separate part of me as it created chaos with words and images.

As the disaster scenarios of my mind unfolded one after another, and the voices of fear proved impossible to ignore, I was shocked. A bigger shock occurred when I realized they had always been there, chattering away. My silence had not created them but had quieted me down enough so I could hear what was previously below my consciousness. This was the key to shifting my mind from disaster to clarity.

My silence forced me to simply witness my thoughts and my reaction to them. I noticed when I paid attention to them, they got louder, as if they knew they had an audience. When I put my attention elsewhere, the voices lessened in intensity.

Over the next few weeks, I slowly learned to witness without being caught by the fear and worry of my own mind. One moment, I would be comparing myself with someone else and making up a story about how I was failing. The next moment my mind was judging the very person I had compared myself with. I started losing faith that my mind always acted in my best interest. If I was not aware, I believed what my mind was telling me. As I became more conscious of the dramas, I could see they were not the truth.

Witnessing the voices without giving them any extra energy (they had plenty on their own, thank you!) taught me many things about my mind. When you witness your own perceptions, you harness a great force of change. When you become conscious of the mind's stories, and witness them objectively, you are empowered to consciously choose what you want to believe instead of running on automatic pilot. At first it may be painful to see the fullness of your mind's chaos. But the recognition of what is not working will lead you to literally change your mind and give it new guidelines.

As I stopped believing my disaster mind, I noticed another voice that spoke to me all the time. It was a quiet, sweet voice that was easily drowned out by negative thinking. When I allowed the negative thinking to pass on through, this voice remained.

The first time I heard this sweeter, compassionate voice, it startled me. I was rushing to get to work and realized I had forgotten something. "Oops, let's go back and get it!" a laughing voice said in my head. I looked around, confused.

Where was my judge? Where was the familiar voice that told me how bad I was? This new voice connected me with my intuition and with a great sense of love and acceptance for myself and everyone around me.

seeing your own disaster mind

By playing a simple game, you can begin to see the nature of your own mind.

To play this game, take a day to listen to your own negative disaster mind. Notice all the ways that you judge yourself and others. Explore all the ways you feel victimized by the world, all the ways you believe you are not enough, or are too much. Allow your negative mind to be consciously present in this moment. What do you judge yourself about? How do you treat yourself when you make a mistake? Does your mind live in the past, the present, or the future? Where do you doubt yourself or feel inadequate in your life?

The mind gets stuck in thinking it sees reality, when it is really only looking through veils of mistaken agreements. Disaster mind, a mind tangled in old agreements, cannot see what is real. If you make the agreement "Mom loves my brother more than me," you will believe it fully, no matter how much evidence there is that your mom, in fact, loves you very much. Then disaster mind takes this agreement and tangles it up even further: "Mom doesn't love me. No one loves me. I am unlovable." What you end up with is a very messy mind, perceiving all sorts of unrealities and believing they are true.

To truly support yourself, learn to look closely at how you motivate or defeat yourself with every step.

makinç the transition to clear perception

Each of us, as individuals, as communities, and on a global level, is in a period of transition. Whether you are learning a new skill for your job, working to release an old belief you have uncovered, starting a new romance, recovering from an addiction, or choosing to take care of your body in a new way, learning to use the mind in a supportive role will ease any change. When you are trapped in disaster mind it is as if the house of your being is being buffeted by a tornado. You cower in the basement or rage at the storm. When you calm your disaster mind, it is like a gentle spring breeze blowing away the dust and cobwebs. Calling on the element of air provides the support you need to bring into your life the following scaffolding:

☀ Patience   ☀ Love
☀ Compassion   ☀ Acceptance
☀ A "You can do it!" attitude   ☀ A safe space
☀ Encouragement   ☀ Humor

Remember that during the shift from disaster mind to positive mind, you will need tremendous patience, humor, and encouragement. Whenever a negative thought arises, simply witness it. Do your best to not judge yourself. Notice what happens when you think negatively. How does your body feel? Where does your mind take you when it goes into fear?

There are four main pitfalls to pay attention to as you let go of your disaster mind: punishment, perfectionism, irresponsibility and over-responsibility.

You need a safe space to practice taking down your old structure. Making mistakes is a part of the process. Punishing yourself with pointed words and stabs is not very helpful. Practice praising yourself instead of hurting yourself when you make a mistake.

Another pitfall to watch out for is perfectionism. Usually we try to be perfect to avoid the punishment we then dole out to ourselves. But imagine living a life where you try to never make a mistake. When we spend our energy trying not to make mistakes, our walking becomes stilted and tight. We constantly look around ourselves to see if anyone is watching. We feel that to be adequate, we must be perfect. Our mind is always ready to tell us how we are doing everything wrong, and it constantly judges and compares us with others: "See, they never make mistakes."

This sort of perfectionism is a horrible way to live. If you expect yourself to be perfect at everything you do, you stifle your creativity and sense of adventure. All sense of fun and spontaneity disappears. It is like trying to live in a vacuum with all the air sucked out. To deconstruct any detrimental perfectionism in yourself, start consciously celebrating your mistakes. Invite yourself to honor your imperfections. Soon you will see that they are not imperfections after all, but a part of the wholeness of a growing, maturing being.

I am a recovering perfectionist. Without awareness of my behaviors, I strove to be perfect in every way. I judged myself for every mistake. I worried that others would see I was not always perfect. I compared myself with people I thought were perfect. My dear friend Gini continued to point out to me the toll my need to be perfect was having on me. She started teasing me whenever I tried to be perfect. Gradually, I learned to tease myself.

I regularly lead spiritual journeys to other countries to help people step out of their old structures. One day at the pyramids of Teotihuacán, Mexico, I invited a group to share their worst-case scenarios—what their disaster minds really believed. I decided to include myself in this exercise, and I found myself saying, "If I am not perfect, no one will like me." Others shared their negative beliefs: "No one is ever going to love me. I am unlovable." "I am broken. No matter how much I want to heal, I never will." "I am never going to be good enough."

We agreed to tease each other for the rest of the day based on these worst fears.

"I know I am not perfect, and you are never going to like me, but can I walk with you?"

"Well, I am broken and I am never going to heal, so I guess it is okay to be with someone imperfect like you."

"I knew it! I am never going to be good enough to climb the pyramid. You all are so much stronger than I am. I can't do it."

"You are right; you're not good enough. But will you love me if I help you climb?"

It was incredibly freeing to clearly see and admit what our fears were, and to make fun of them. Today my apprentices are great allies in helping me see if I am slipping back into perfectionism. As a community, we practice honesty and support one another in moving beyond our old stories and beliefs. We encourage clear perception by taking responsibility for our thoughts, and by not taking them so seriously.

Honesty and humor are amazing antidotes for the disease of disaster mind. When you laugh at your own mind and find it silly, it loses its ferocious power. As the mind surrenders to supporting your whole being rather than being right about its old agreements, clarity emerges. Awareness allows you to uncover the unconscious agreements that take you away from center. You learn to discern the truth rather than judge what you do not like.

Another way we hurt ourselves is by being irresponsible or by being overly responsible. Responsibility is tricky. You can stunt your own growth in two ways: by asking other people to carry you, and by carrying others. Pay attention to the situations where you do not take responsibility for your own journey, but also notice the flip side—the situations where you take responsibility for someone else's journey.

Trust that when others fall down, they will figure out how to get themselves up again. Share with them all of your love, support, faith, encouragement. But keep your focus on your own journey, on picking yourself up with love and faith, and letting others do the same for themselves.

Giving others the space to find their own feet is not easy. I experienced the importance of putting faith in other people's ability to take self-responsibility from one of my students.

Robert is a young, creative man in my community who moved to Berkeley from Arizona several years ago. For the first six months or so, he struggled to find a place to live, to secure a job he liked, and to manage his finances. At first we were all happy to support his new life in Berkeley. He borrowed money from several different people and slept on many couches. I let him take classes for free, or for work-trade.

His life continued to be chaotic. He constantly found and lost both housing and jobs. After months of no real improvement, I inquired into his background. He owed many people money in Arizona, and had basically tapped out his resources in his former community.

I called him and we had a long talk about personal responsibility and the importance of creating stability for himself. I pointed out that we had supported him as best we could, but I now believed we were disempowering him by catching him every time he fell. I knew it would be hard, but we both agreed it was time for him to learn to catch himself.

Our community made an agreement to stop loaning him money. He would need to pay for all of his classes. We encouraged him to focus completely on stability—to find a good living situation and a job that supported him. He courageously decided on his own not to continue in my Advanced

Teacher Training Program, so he could focus his energy on his own survival issues.

It was challenging for me personally to tell him no. Each time Robert asked to borrow just a little bit of money to pay rent, or to sleep at the Toltec Center, I asked him to rely on his own resources. At one point he ended up in a homeless shelter, and then lived in transitional housing. My mind kept telling me that I should feel guilty for not helping someone when I had the resources to do so, that I was hurting Robert, that I was a bad person. I kept focusing on my greater desire to support Robert in a new way.

Despite my fearful thoughts, I was able to consciously witness my mind throughout this process. This allowed me to stay open to Robert. I encouraged him to find stability in his life by choosing a job he felt comfortable with, and putting all his attention on keeping it. The extremity of his situation forced him to realize the importance of taking care of himself. He found a stable job, and eventually located housing that he could afford and that nurtured him. He later thanked me for my support and faith in him.

There will be times when simply witnessing your mind, with no judgment or need, will give you the awareness to shift your focus, to choose where you want to put your mind and actions. Other times you will need to consciously shift your perspective from one thought or belief to another, over and over again.

So, you can see that your first steps on the journey back to center have to do with the falling down and getting up of learning to see clearly, without judgment. When you cultivate the excitement of the child, you celebrate every little victory. Invite your mind to become curious in your perception rather than demanding.

Learning to make a change in your life takes a fair amount of ruthlessness, along with compassion. When you take the easy way out by saying, "I don't want to fall down, so I am going to stop trying," or "You can walk better than I can, so why don't you carry me?" you soon find your legs have atrophied. You might wake up one day to find you spent the last ten years hiding behind others or escaping from your own dreams and potential.

Clear perception allows you to walk freely, without worrying whether you are making a mistake. You start using all your experiences to benefit your growth, rather than to punish yourself.

stopping disaster mind in its tracks

Proper grammar is a great strategy for disarming the might of disaster mind. Like most of us, you probably have a tendency to make huge run-on sentences of judgment upon judgment. Once you learn why it's not helpful to judge yourself, you discover that when you are judging yourself you get disappointed, angry, or ashamed. You then link your judgments to how others may be judging you, or compare yourself with others. "These pants don't fit me very well, my thighs are too fat, oh if only I had the willpower to stop eating so much sugar then my thighs and butt wouldn't be so big, and if only

I worked out more, like Christy, my body would be okay like hers, her body is so beautiful, and mine is so ugly that no one is going to want to date me, so why am I even bothering to try on new pants, they are not going to hide the fact that I am ugly and that no one loves me, that I am all alone and am never going to be appreciated for who I am because I live in a society that judges people who are bigger than a size 4, and I was never a size 4, no matter how much I dieted, though maybe if I was better at dieting my thighs wouldn't be so big and I wouldn't be so unhappy all the time..."

When you catch yourself judging yourself for judging yourself, or comparing yourself with others, put a period in the sentence at the first opportunity. "These pants don't fit me." Period. Now create a new sentence, a new paragraph, that supports you with a new thought: "My thighs are the thighs of a grown woman, not the thighs of a teenager." Or "I am looking forward to working out and getting my body in shape." Notice if you judged yourself, and notice how it affected you. "Ah, I just judged myself for having fat thighs, and ended up hating myself." Now bring in the kind hands of a parent encouraging a child to take another step. Shift your perspective away from judging yourself and toward acceptance and love.

With our eyes we shift our perspective thousands of times a day. Raise a finger about four inches in front of your eyes and focus on it completely. Now shift your focus to something in the distance. Notice how your finger is still there, but it is only a tiny part of a much bigger framework. We can do the same perspective shift with our judging mind as we move into our witnessing mind.

The judge—our negative mind—sees things in terms of black and white. Instead of simply being aware that a certain plant will make you sick if you eat it, the judge says, "That plant is bad," simplifying and judging a plant that may be beneficial in other circumstances. Below are examples of judging mind vs. witnessing mind:

JUDGE: That person is bad. (Often with: Therefore I am good.)
WITNESS: I do not feel comfortable around that person.

JUDGE: I am worthless and undesirable.
WITNESS: I am feeling vulnerable and weak today.

JUDGE: I keep judging and fighting with my boss. She makes me feel like a terrible person. She is unreasonable and uncaring.
WITNESS: I need to stay out of my boss's way when she is angry, or I tend to get angry myself and make things worse. Her moods do not have any thing to do with me. She seems to get angry most often in the mornings. I will practice being kind.

JUDGE: My thighs are fat. I'm never going to find someone to love me.
WITNESS: I'm not happy with my body right now. Am I comparing myself with how I think I should be? Am I making up stories about what others will think?

Using the witness, we train ourselves to stop listening to the judge and victim as our only sources of information. We open our vision to include all the resources in our being. When we truly witness this vast sky of the mind, we find silence and peace. We are conscious of the stormy thoughts below, but our attention is fixed on the expansiveness of our awareness, not on the endless dramas of disaster mind. When we learn to rest the mind in this place of soft witnessing, the judge and victim dissolve like mist into a flow of acceptance.

By cultivating the witness, you learn to allow what is. By allowing what is, you naturally step into acceptance. When acceptance motivates your actions, you forgive yourself for your perceived faults and imperfections. Your choices are guided by love. They come from a wider perception of body, emotions, and life force in balance with the tool of the mind.

As your perception clears, you become your own loving parent, your own best friend and mentor. You become the artist of your own life. You can now create a new framework from which you live and breathe—a fresh structure in which you maintain your center.

Becoming the artist of your Life

When you judge, you polarize what you perceive and do not leave space for magic and love. A beautiful Chinese saying reminds me of the power of being in the moment with no judgments: "Now that my barn has burned to the ground, I can more easily see the moon."

To shift your perception, consciously become an artist, an architect of love. Artists can look at a rundown shack that is falling apart and see beyond the debris to the gem within. A true artist does not ignore what is and only fantasize about what could be, but recognizes and is excited about the work ahead.

You are a work in progress. You have been trained to live outside of your center. Wherever you are on your journey inward, be compassionate. Every time you judge or compare yourself with others, you are taking a step backward. Watch for it, but be kind to yourself about it, too. Remember your choice to be an artist who creates, rather than a critic who destroys.

With your perception, you can use what you see to hurt or heal. Therefore, getting your perception in alignment is a high priority. Again, this takes time and patience and plenty of falling down and getting up. Be gentle and persistent with yourself. All of the elements and their gifts will guide you to clearer perception. As you embody each of them, you will learn the art of moving yourself toward healing rather than toward further emotional or mental suffering.

Clear perception allows us pull back and witness the mind with a curious eye. Curiosity and a good dose of humor are the best antidotes for the serious, self-absorbed modern mind. The art of seeing with new eyes allows us to simply look at the limiting structure of our agreements, without reinforcing it. The next element in our circle, fire, will teach us how to clean and clear out the old agreements that block our magic.

practices

MIND EXPLORATION

Spend a week noticing how you perceive yourself. What eyes do you use as you watch yourself? If you were a child learning to walk, what would you be saying to yourself? Keep a record of your perceptions about yourself. You can use index cards or a little notebook, or even a tape recorder to record impressions in the moment. Do your best to witness, to be an explorer looking at new, interesting terrain. There is nothing you need to do or change this week. You are gathering information.

If you find you are judging yourself for your perceptions, remember grammar and punctuation: "Period!" Stop any run-on sentences emanating from your judging self. Pretend you are witnessing the mind of your dearest, most beloved friend. Bring all of your compassion and clarity to this task.

Make three columns. In the first column, take quick notes of what you perceive, without thinking or analyzing them:

perception

"I am going to be late for work. I am bad."

"I hate my hair."

"I look old."

"I am excited about my date tonight."

"What if he doesn't like me?"		
"I am tired of this job."		
"Maria is selfish and uncaring."		
"I am angry at myself for not standing up for myself."		
"I wish I were more like Brian."		

At the end of each day, go back over your notes and mark in the second column which comments support you and take you toward your center, and which are based on fear judgment, comparison, feeling victimized, and so on. Note if you see core agreements that might stem from old childhood beliefs. What are you really saying to yourself?

perception	based on
"I am going to be late for work. I am bad."	*Fear, core agreement*
"I hate my hair."	*Comparison*
"I look old."	*Comparison*
"I am excited about my date tonight."	*Center*
"What if he doesn't like me?"	*Fear, core agreement*

"I am tired of this job."	*Perhaps support or judgment, depending*
"Maria is selfish and uncaring."	*Judgment*
"I am angry at myself for not standing up for myself."	*Victimized*
"I wish I were more like Brian."	*Comparison*

Go through your entire list, and in the third column rewrite your perception, imagining you are teaching yourself to walk. You might find that you write the exact same words, but the energy of the words is very different. Can you discern and support rather than judge? Take responsibility for how you feel.

PERCEPTION	BASED ON	RE-WRITE
"I am going to be late for work. I am bad."	*Fear, core agreement*	*I did not leave myself enough time to get ready. Tomorrow I will set my alarm earlier so I do not have to rush.*
"I hate my hair."	*Comparison*	*My hair is curlier than usual today.*
"I look old."	*Comparison*	*My skin is changing.*

"I am excited about my date tonight.	Center	
"What if he doesn't like me?"	Fear, core agreement	I wonder if we will get along?
"I am tired of this job."	Perhaps support, or judgement, depending.	How can I bring more excitement to this job?
"Maria is selfish and uncaring."	Judgment	My stomach knots up when Maria is curt.
"I am angry at myself for not standing up for myself."	Victimized	I feel small and power-less, and then I get angry at myself when I don't speak my truth.
"I wish I were more like Brian."	Comparison	I like Brian's honesty.

Remember, this is an exercise to track old beliefs and current ways of thinking. It is not a means of judging yourself for your judgments! It is a way for you to look at your mind and notice where you can shift your perception. You can use this exercise to make yourself suffer more, by judging yourself, or you can use it as an exploration of disaster mind. Please do your best to witness and be curious rather than attacking yourself further!

SHOWING UP IN THIS MOMENT

Another way we can clear our perception is by coming into the present moment. To explore what your mind is up to, spend fifteen minutes sitting quietly, watching your thoughts. Get a piece of paper and make three columns. Mark them past, present, future. Close your eyes, and let your mind go. Notice your thoughts. When a thought about the past arises, make a mark in the past column. When you are in the present, make a mark in the present column. When you find yourself in the future, make a mark in the future column.

When you are done, count up each column and put a percentage for each at the bottom. Do this exercise once a week for a month, and see if you can begin to train your mind to stay more in the present. This takes practice and encouragement. Remember, your mind is learning to walk in the present. Support yourself in this new skill. Be a loving parent to yourself. Here are examples of past, present, and future thinking:

past	pResent	futuRe
I forgot to buy mayonnaise.	It is warm in this room.	I wonder what Fred will do if he gets the job he wants?
A memory of being betrayed by your best friend when you were twelve.	Appreciating your breath	Dreaming about what you will say on your next date with George.
I wonder if I did that project correctly.	I am grateful to have finished my project.	Will I get a raise if the project I completed is well received?
Replaying a past discussion over and over in your head.	I did the best I could in my talk with Liz.	Liz is going to misinterpret what I said and tell her friends.

CONNECTING WITH THE ELEMENT OF AIR

The shift from disaster mind to clear perception is made up of a million little acts of awareness, combined with the action of shifting your focus over and over again. Consciously connecting with the element of air will support you in making this shift.

Start by going through your home and opening every window. Invite the wind to blow in and clear out any old habitual perceptions and cyclical thoughts. As you open each window, say out loud what you would like to shift in your perception. Here are some examples:

"I invite the wind in to blow away my fears about the future, and to remind me to slow down and come back to enjoying the present moment."

"As I open this window, I open to a new perspective in my life."

"May the winds of change breathe new vision into my life. I release my judgmental thoughts and invite in clarity."

You can repeat one sentence over and over again at each window, or say something new. You might even write down your sentences and tape them to one or more window sills, so in the future each time you open a window you are reminded of your new perception.

As you do this practice, keep your awareness in this moment, and feel the wind moving through your house. Invite the wind to move through all the rooms, bringing fresh perspective and blowing away any confusion, lack of vision, or tangled thoughts.

Stand in the middle of your home and breathe this fresh air into your being. Use your own connection to air, your breath, to release any stuck thoughts and bring yourself into the present moment. Intentionally breathe more clarity and space into your mind and body.

In the future when you are feeling muddled or confused, go back to this feeling of wind against your skin. Imagine opening a window inside of your being and letting the air blow away the fear and judgments of disaster mind.

Feng shui, the Asian practice of creating harmony in one's environment, focuses on the placement of the elements. Before any sacred structure was built, ancient peoples aligned the building with each of the elements, to bolster and bless the new structure. Today, people around the world use the natural elements of feng shui to bring clarity and prosperity to their living and work spaces.

INNER GUIDANCE

AIR VISUALIZATION TO CREATE A NEW CONTAINER

Visualization is a great technique to help you create new pathways in the mind and body. When we visualize something in our minds, we energize it and make it real. We call on invisible forces to support and guide us. Shamans have used visualization and spiritual journeying for centuries to connect with allies and gain information.

This visualization is a powerful way to bring the teachings from the Dream of the Elders into your own life.

o help create your new structure, you can call in a guardian from each of the four elements to remind you of the new qualities you are embodying. The first guardian is from the element of air. From the air you learn the art of clear perception, and the right use of your mind.

1) Let your body be comfortable, and take some deep breaths into your belly.

2) Imagine yourself standing in the middle of a beautiful stone circle. This circle encompasses and holds all of you in its embrace. Facing one direction, ask for guidance and vision from the element of air, to help you perceive yourself clearly.

3) Invite an air guide to join you and help you see with new eyes. Be open to how that guide may appear. Your air guide may be an animal, a person you know, or a stranger. It may be a quiet voice in your head, or a knowing in your body. Your guardian of air may not come to you immediately, but later in a dream or while you are in the middle of your day this guide may appear. The wind may come whisper in your ear. Pray for the seeds of a new structure to sprout, so you may feel supported as you dissolve the old ways of seeing and being.

4) When you feel complete, ask for a symbol to represent this new anchor, and place it in one direction of your circle.

o further support yourself, you can build an altar to represent your journey. Choose an object to represent your centered self, and surround it with stones or beads or objects to represent your circle of acceptance for what is. As you call in each of your guardians, pick an object to represent this guardian and place it on the outside of the circle. A feather or a pair of glasses, or any object that pleases you can represent air and your new vision. Set your intent to use all of the elements and their gifts to guide you through your fears and old beliefs, through disaster mind, back to your center.

All the means of action—the shapeless masses—the materials—lie everywhere about us. What we need is the celestial fire to change the flint into the transparent crystal, bright and clear. That fire is genius.

Henry Wadsworth Longfellow
(1807 - 1882)

Cleaning anything involves making something else dirty, but anything can get dirty without something else getting clean.

Laurence J. Peter (1919 - 1988)

FIRE

the art of cleaning

ire represents our spirit and the energetic aspect of our being. The second element in our circle, fire teaches us about the wisdom of cleaning.

Our spirit is the unique essence of who we are. For the Toltec, each human is a specific ray of light, an individual vibration of energy. Our physical body is the visible part of our being. Our spirit, the invisible part of us, can also be called our energetic body. Our energetic body flows through and around our physical body. Our energetic body communicates with and receives information from a variety of sources. It shares this information with our mental, emotional, and physical bodies.

Agreements, especially the unconscious agreements we made as children, clutter our energetic body and bog us down. When we make an agreement, it eventually becomes a static structure in our energetic bodies that saps our vitality. These structures cause us to perceive the world in ways that reinforce our beliefs. They also cause confusion among our energetic, mental, emotional, and physical bodies.

Although the process may be explained differently, clearing our perceptions and cleaning unwanted structures are shared by all spiritual and psychological paths. We start the journey hopeful or desperate, but we are rarely prepared for the intensity of the debris we have to navigate. Often we sabotage ourselves when any real change begins to take place.

When I first started investigating my thoughts, I was horrified by what I found. Here I was, a supposedly spiritual person with heaps of judgment, fear, and stagnant beliefs in my unconscious. I spent a great deal of time judging myself before I accomplished any actual cleaning. Eventually, I saw that any time I spent judging myself was like tracking mud all over my house while complaining loudly about the dirt. Having clear perception allowed me to take off my muddy shoes first, then investigate what I wanted to keep and what I wanted to clear away in my house.

OPENING THE DOOR TO CLEANING

Imagine yourself as a house you keep fairly clean for the outside world. By keeping your house clean, you get approval and acceptance from the outside world. Every house has a closet, and in yours you stuff everything you do not like about yourself: all the unconscious agreements, inner voices, and behaviors that have been passed down to you from your family. When you invite people over, you are friendly until they get anywhere near your closet.

"Don't open that!" you say with a threatening look. You do not want anyone to see what lurks behind the closed doors.

Or maybe you are a person who invites others over and immediately drags them to your closet. "Look at all of this! Can you believe it? It is so awful!" Comparing closets has now become a hobby for some people.

In either case, one day you decide it is time to clean out the closet. Maybe you read a book that says it is a good idea. Maybe you are in so much pain you are willing to do anything to feel better.

If you are really going to clean out a closet, what do you need to do?

First, you show your willingness by opening the door.

Second, you must have the tenacity to pull everything out of the closet so you can see what is in there. This is where many people stumble.

What happens to your nice, clean, presentable house when you pull everything out of that musty back closet? Everything that was hidden and tucked neatly away is suddenly out in the open, strewn all over the rooms of your life. What seemed like a really good idea—pulling everything out of the closet—is now messing up your house.

You might get overwhelmed. You might blame others. You might tell yourself, "See, I am really messed up. No one else could possibly have this much stuff." Suddenly, the path you are on is wrong, your teacher is no good, or you are beyond all possible hope. Your reaction to this new, very obvious mess might be to look around and say, "Okay, this is not working!" The temptation is to immediately shove everything back into the closet.

When you choose to truly clean out what no longer serves you, you must be willing to open the door on some not-so-pleasant thoughts, emotions, and bodily sensations. This is why clear perception is so crucial. Otherwise, you will judge what is inside and end up creating more dirt. Before you can open the closet door, you need to be curious about what is inside, and willing to sift through the garbage to find the truth. You learn to be willing to feel out of control, to be unclear about what is yours and what is not, and to be confused, all without judging yourself.

If you open the doors to untangle your structure, and your perception is still trapped in disaster mind, you will only create more chaos. When your mind is clear, you can look on the chaos with a sense of humor: "Wow, that is in my closet?" Instead of becoming depressed at the piles of behaviors you have pulled into the light, you are excited to reclaim what is real and leave the rest behind.

Pulling everything out of your closet allows choice. Your clear mind keeps you from judging what you find. To be even more accurate, your clear mind notices what you judge and what you feel victimized by, without believing either. Everything that arises is a chance to dismantle your old structure.

When your thoughts are laid out in front of you, you can begin to sort through what belongs to you and what does not. Following the closet analogy, you will find old clothes that do not fit you anymore and old beliefs that do not serve you. You will find things given to you that you never really liked, but did not know how to refuse. You will find whole structures that were passed on from your ancestors. Can you cultivate a new attitude—"Check this out! What an interesting thing to believe!"—instead of, "I am a failure. Look at this mess. It proves I am bad."

You spent your entire lifetime building the structures that limit you. The remodeling process takes time and repeated intentional action. The fire element is about action. After we witness through the eyes of air, we move into cleaning what is no longer true. Even if you are not sure exactly how it will happen, as you clean your happiness, energy, and integrity will be uncovered. Just remember, cleaning is not something you do once in your life, and then it is over. Action is about practice.

two types of cleaning

One of the first times I was aware of cleaning my thoughts was in a bookstore in Berkeley.

It was a lazy day, and I was engaged in one of my favorite activities—browsing through books. I hung out in the self-help section, reading titles, enjoying the colors and texture of covers and paper, flipping through the books that looked interesting.

When I went to my car, I noticed that my energy level had plummeted. I felt bad without knowing why. I stopped everything and sat in my car, tracking what had happened.

Moving backward in time, I noticed how joyous I had been in the bookstore. As I witnessed more deeply, I saw myself in front of the self-help books and heard a voice that I had not noticed in the moment: "Look at all these books. All these people have been published. You are never going to write a book. And if you do, no one will read it. Everything has been written already. You don't have what it takes to write."

As I became quiet within myself I made space for what was troubling me to arise and present itself. By bringing this voice into my conscious mind, I was able clean it out by not believing it. I knew that it was connected to deeper fears, but at that moment all I needed to do was clear out that old thought and go on with my day. I told myself, "You will write many books because your heart wants to." My energy lifted, I felt happy again, and off I went.

In my mind I made a little note. I had just done a short-term cleaning around a fear of writing. Underneath this was a deeper fear, which I put in my long-term cleaning pile. This pile stemmed back to one big fear: not getting approval and ultimately not being loved.

I helped myself in two ways that day. The first way was by paying attention to my energy and clearing out a disaster mind thought. The second way was by witnessing that my fear of writing was a larger part of my structure, related to needing outside validation.

Before tackling long-term cleaning, it helps to develop the skill of short-term cleaning. I was able to clear out my disaster mind thoughts and enjoy the rest of my day because of years of practice with short-term cleaning. Short-term cleaning includes the general pickup, dusting, and washing of everyday life. Long-term cleaning entails our larger renovations that take dedicated focus and space.

SHORT-TERM CLEANING

Dirt obscures your center. When you physically clean, you remove the debris and clutter that hides the essence of the truth. Fear and self-doubt are clutter. They will arise as you make new choices. With every new action, you open a door within you. Behind that door lies both your integrity and any fears you stashed there as a child.

When you picture your energetic structure as a house, you can see how the nooks and crannies get dirty. When you are not looking, dust bunnies grow under the beds, and dirt piles up in unexpected places.

Short-term cleaning is about watching where you collect dirt in your system, and each day clearing it out.

Imagine if you washed your dishes or your car one time and said, "Okay, I am done with that job. I never have to do it again." Or if you dusted your house one time, and then became furious that it became dusty again. "How dare it get dusty again? I just dusted!" This sort of short-term cleaning can seem repetitive and trivial, but it is crucial.

One thing you can guarantee is that dirt happens. Both our physical world and our internal energetic world need daily cleaning and polishing. We know the importance of brushing our teeth daily, of washing our hands on a regular basis. Our energetic being is no different. It, too, accumulates dirt and grime from use.

Our energetic structure similarly snags energy in the rough places. If part of your old structure tells the story "My mother doesn't love me," which has transformed into "I am not lovable," then each time you see the hint of an "I am not lovable" situation, it creates an emotional reaction within you; it snags you. You might see two people embracing and unconsciously think, "See, they have love, but I do not, because I am not lovable." The place within you that feels unlovable now has more dirt piled on top of it.

When dirt collects in your system, your energy decreases. You may find yourself thinking about something over and over again, or feeling exhausted. This is the time to stop and check in with yourself. "Is there something I need to clean in this moment?"

Take the above incident. You see a couple embracing and you notice yourself starting to judge yourself for not being in a relationship. Or you are aware of feeling drained and tired, or you realize you are angry. Take a moment to acknowledge what you are thinking or feeling, to witness what is going on for you.

Now, imagine disconnecting your experience from the couple's experience. You are having an experience based on your own dirt, not on their reality. Bless them, and take responsibility for the energy inside of you.

Imagine cleaning out your energy. Your imagination is powerful. It can help to move and direct energy. You can use the image of a broom, or of fire, to cleanse and release whatever does not serve you in this moment. Any image will work. The more real you make the image, the more effective it will be.

Then invite in a new thought to clear out what you do not need and bring in what you do in a creative way. Ask yourself, "What is the truth?" You may realize, "Oh, that's right, I am choosing not to be in relationship right now!" or "I miss being intimate with someone. I am going to ask my best friend for a hug and to go for a walk with me."

The act of pulling everything out of your closet and witnessing will teach you a great deal about what type of dirt you like to collect. Use this information to put daily cleaning into practice. Start with the small things; move onto the large.

Be aware that there may be a gap between a reaction you have, your perception of it, and the action to clean it. For my bookstore incident, my ability to locate and clean my negative perceptions in about five minutes was an acquired skill. Prior to this breakthrough, it would often take days or weeks before I noticed my energy was low and that I was judging myself or feeling victimized about an event.

As you pay attention to your energy levels, you will learn about your own patterns. This will give you the information you need for cleaning. For example, I noticed a pattern of major "dirt" arising inside of me a couple of days after I made an important decision. I had registered for a very exciting workshop that was also very expensive. I knew it would change my life. For two days I was joyous and had no doubt I was making the right decision. On the third day my energy plummeted. I was depressed, doubtful, and cynical. I knew I had made the wrong decision. "What was I thinking? I cannot do this workshop at this time in my life! I do not have enough money, or time, or energy. What if I cannot pay my rent next month? What if I do not like the workshop?" I allowed my dire thoughts to pull me off-center.

In the middle of my despair I realized, "Maybe these thoughts are not real, but a backlash of fear." I made a note to pay attention the next time I made a positive, big decision in my life. And sure enough, three days after my next big life change, I went into fear and doubt. But this time I was conscious of the cycle. Because I was now aware of the pattern, I was able to accept these emotions for what they were: dirt. I had sponge and mop ready to clear it out. I took a long, soapy bath, and imagined all my old fears and disaster thoughts going down the drain with my dirty bath water. Soon I was excited about my life and my choices again.

Cleaning allows for authentic centering. The practices at the end of this chapter will help you learn about your patterns and improve your short-term cleaning abilities. They will guide you to hold more energy and prepare for long-term cleaning.

LONG-TERM CLEANING

The core agreements you made as a child will take a while to dissolve because they are a part of a much greater societal structure. You do not need to judge yourself or feel bad that you have core agreements such as needing love and approval, feeling you are bad, or fearing that you are going to be abandoned. Of course you have these agreements. It is the way we all are trained.

Long-term cleaning projects, such as a core belief like "I need to be perfect to be okay," are best saved until you have the energy and time to dedicate to them. By constantly perceiving and clearing out what attaches to your structure, it is easier to track and monitor the deeper core agreements. Long-term means long-term.

Put things into perspective by counting up how many years you have been acting from a core belief in your life. If you have lived your life believing you are not lovable or that you are undeserving, it will take some time to clean all the manifestations of these beliefs. Don't be surprised when these issues keep appearing in your life, even long after you think you are done with them!

One thing I have discovered about our emotional closets is that they have trapdoors. Just when you think you have cleaned out a particular issue or structure, it seems to pop up again in a slightly different form. This points to a long-term cleaning issue. When you make space in your closet, the deeper issues then have room to emerge into the light.

When you are in disaster mind and a trapdoor opens with more stuff, you say, "Not again! I just cleaned that. I must be doing this wrong." When you come from clear mind, you are interested in this new appearance, whatever it is, and know that you are discovering a vast, hidden chamber within. Cleaning becomes exciting because you know you are gathering the strength and vision to act on the foundational pieces that keep you out of balance. By not letting the debris of current events pile up, and by keeping track of the long-term projects, you will gather energy.

takiN$ responsibility

When we are not aware, it seems that most of our problems stem from outside ourselves. The cleaning that needs to be done seems external: "If only my boss would not yell at me." "If only my wife would listen to me." "If only the world wasn't such a messed up place." We may focus on trying to change and control the external to make ourselves feel better. But by opening the closet wide, we discover that anything that appears external is actually an internal need for cleaning.

When you take honest responsibility for your emotional reactions and your opinions, you see that your responses about others needing to change are cover-ups for where you either need to change or move on. Your emotional reactions to current events often have nothing at all to do with the present moment, but are governed by what still needs to be cleaned from the past.

Robert's story from the previous chapter shows the far-reaching transformation that can happen when one person makes the shift to internal cleaning. From Robert's point of view, he was a victim of outside circumstances. He would be able to get on his feet if only someone would have faith in him. He just needed a little time, a little money, a little help. He blamed others for not giving him what he needed.

Before I took responsibility for my old beliefs around needing to take care of others, I believed Robert's victim story. My thinking was a loop that was no longer served me or anyone around me. The truth was that Robert had what he needed to change his life. The major problem was that I had somehow associated rescuing others with being loving. Anytime I perceived that someone around me might need help, an old pattern would be triggered inside of me. If I did help I would feel useful, and therefore loved. If I did not help, I felt bad about myself and guilty. The cycle would never stop as long as I needed to be helpful to feel okay about myself.

When I made the space for Robert to take responsibility for securing the resources he needed to live, he also began to take responsibility for his own sense of happiness and love. If I had continued to rescue him, he might still be relying on others for his sense of security. By stopping my own cycle of needing to take care of others to feel loved, I was able to really love and support Robert, not out of guilt or for my own needs, but out of genuine compassion.

Do not fall into the trap of using your actions to clean up other people's stuff. Such efforts may seem a lot easier in the short-term but help no one in the long-term. This may be your first area of cleaning—pulling your energy back to your own house! Right use of action is about taking responsibility for what is yours to clean. It can be easy to notice that your partner, or your boss, or your parents have full closets and dust bunnies under their sofas. If they invite you to share what you see, do so with utmost love and respect. Then create the space and encouragement for them to do their own cleaning.

cLeaninG as aRt, cLeaninG as pRayeR

You can bring love and joy to your cleaning projects, or you can bring discouragement and annoyance. Notice how you clean your physical house. Is this a reflection of the energy that you bring to your internal cleaning? When dirty dishes pile up, do you put on music and dance while you do them, or do you wash them grudgingly, wishing they would go away? Do you take the time in your life to keep things neat, or do you rush around, always a little behind?

Sometimes cleaning is about letting the debris settle. If you go in with a blowtorch, determined to clear out everything right now, you will create more chaos than cleaning. If you have been triggered by something and are emotionally stirred up, allowing the dust to settle and the emotions to simmer down enables you to see clearly where to best put your energy. Patience will guide you to right use of action.

Cleaning of all forms can be a prayer. Each time I wash my dishes or scrub the floors, I honor the power of cleaning and am grateful for all the gifts in my life. Every time I place soap on my hands, I link it to the cleaning I am doing in my mind. Even when physical cleaning feels overwhelming, I start at one spot of a room and bless each object I touch. Instead of looking at the whole, I focus on the one area of this moment, and keep working until it is completed—all in gratitude.

Your structures, whether you like them or not, have served you in some way. You built your energetic structures to help you comprehend and manage your world. While you clean your old agreements and beliefs, thank them for all the ways that they have served you then dismantle them piece by piece. Wash off the dirt of your judgments and the need for things to be other than they are. To avoid being overwhelmed by the enormity of your task, keep your focus on one area, clear as much as you can, and then move on. Gratitude and perseverance are the best form of elbow grease there is. Explore the beauty of what you are cleaning, and its perfection, as you release it.

tHe gRemLINs IN tHe cLoset

One of the games I use to bring humor to the sometimes intense work of cleaning is to personalize the forces that thwart change. I visualize them as small, green gremlins.

Gremlins are the guardians of your structure, and they will do anything to keep it intact. As you sort and clean your closet, gremlins will whisper and shout at you to distract you from your task. Gremlins can serve as your biggest allies because they lead you where you want to go. When one of them shows up shouting, "Don't go that way!" or whispering words of fear in your ears, you know you are actually on the right track.

Here is a list of some different kinds of gremlins. As you clean yourself, keep an eye out for gremlins that disguise themselves as your friends. Listen to them, not for the truth they speak (for they're prone to lie), but for the information they reveal.

Fear: As you get closer to cleaning big agreements and structures, the gremlins of fear will arise, shaking and moaning. Often these reveal you are on the right track. Fear gremlins appear real, but they are really more like smoke—easy to walk through once you get up the courage to do so. A fear gremlin might say, "You are never going to be good enough."

Defensiveness: When you are clean, there is nothing to prove; you just are. If you notice yourself defending a particular viewpoint or belief, pay attention. Often a gremlin is protecting its territory. The statement "I am right!" is a sure sign of this gremlin.

Not wanting to look bad: This is a corollary to defending. In order not to look bad, most of us tend to defend our actions. If you feel your image is at stake, or that you need to appear a certain way to gain approval or respect, pay attention. A gremlin is present. What is the agreement that is prompting your defensive action?

Sleepiness: As you clear out layers of debris and old agreements, you uncover the core foundations that keep you trapped. Gremlins will jump in and wave their wands in front of your eyes: "You are very sleepy. There is nothing here. Rest and forget everything." At such moments rest may be fine, but keep your awareness intact so when you wake up you will get right back on track. A healthy amount of denial is okay at times. Go to a movie to escape your problem, but not necessarily every night.

Huge emotions: Gremlins sometimes will get in and stir, stir, stir all your emotions. If you are having an emotional reaction that is out of proportion with the situation, or appears out of nowhere, slow down and take a couple of deep breaths. Look beyond the current situation to earlier events.

Projecting onto others: This is a favorite gremlin tactic. It most often takes two forms. One: You see and judge the things you do not like about yourself as being the traits of someone else. Two: You think people outside of you are seeing and judging all those things you hate about yourself. The gremlins are delighted when they can get you to project onto someone else or against yourself. For example, "My aunt thinks I am not smart enough to be a real success." In reality, your aunt might be supportive of you, but her support is veiled by the negative self-judgment that you project onto her because of her honesty in helping you identify your obstacle.

Compensating: This is what I call the pendulum tactic. One gremlin whispers, "You are too nice!" So you get mean. Later the gremlin whispers, "You are too mean!" When you are off-center and heading back to balance, a gremlin will invite you to overcompensate, so you are off-balance in exactly the opposite way.

The gremlins of reaction and fear can mirror and guide you to the dirty spots. Get out the mop and broom and joyously go to work! Thank the gremlins when they appear instead of cursing them. Watching your gremlins as you clean will prepare you for the next step on your journey—releasing the gremlins.

As you clear and clean, treat yourself like a favorite child who, after a long day of play, returns home covered in mud, with hair full of snarls and stickers. With all of your compassion, patience, and gentle care, sit yourself down and begin to wash off the mud and comb out the tangles.

Beneath the dirt and ratty hair lies a precious child, ready to love, open, and explore life.

The tribal !Kung people of Africa walk on fire as a means to raise their energy and bring healing to their communities. For the !Kung fire is revered as a means to bring the individual and community into spiritual balance. It represents surrender to a greater force. The shamans of the community blend with the fire by walking or rolling over, or rubbing themselves with coals. They then share this energy by doing hands-on healing with others. Today, thousands of people continue this ancient, global practice of firewalking.

pRactices

DAILY CLEANING: RECAPITULATION

One of the most powerful cleansing techniques is recapitulation. Recapitulation is a simple technique based on breathing and the use of a focused will to reclaim energy. Its purpose is to gather energy that you lost in past interactions. Each day as you interact with the world, you lose some of your own energy and take on the thoughts, beliefs, and energy of others. Your disaster mind creates leaks in your vital energy, and your structure magnetizes familiar dirt. Recapitulation is a process of deliberate internal cleaning and untangling on an energetic level.

Recapitulation is a form of conscious cleaning that frees you from the energetic filaments that connect you to past events of your life. These energetic ties take you out of the moment because whenever you experience similar circumstances these threads are activated, pulling you into the past. Recapitulation reclaims this energy and releases the links to past events.

Reclaiming energy allows you to make dramatic changes in the present. There are different theories about how to do recapitulation. Toltec author Taisha Abelar spent the better part of a year visiting a cave each day and recapitulating her entire life. Victor Sanchez, a Toltec teacher and author, recommends building a box to use for doing all recapitulation work. I used to crawl under my desk to do my recapitulation practice, though now I often do it lying on my bed before I go to sleep, or early in the morning. There are many Toltec books that explain the various recapitulation methods; see the bibliography at the end of this book for other resources.

There are three important parameters for doing a recapitulation: establishing a safe, comfortable, non-distracting space, setting your intent or will to reclaim your energy, and using your breath to pull and reclaim energy. I like to imagine that the energy I am going back to reclaim is pieces of light threads, and I use this visualization to breathe back these filaments into my body.

Whenever you do recapitulation, it is important to come from a place of love and acceptance. What you do not want to do is go back in your memory to a painful time and create more self-wounding, either by reliving all the emotions or by judging yourself or others involved, or by re-analyzing the situation. Your purpose is simply to go back as a witness, with love and forgiveness, and reunite your energy in the present. If you feel emotions or judgment, then you are not ready to clean that particular event. Remember your periods and grammar; do not judge yourself for judging or comparing yourself.

My dear friend Laurence Andrews introduced me to the idea of doing a short, daily recapitulation in the evenings before bed. I call this the five-minute quickie recapitulation technique. It is brief, but very effective on many levels. This recapitulation method teaches you how to review your day and how to gather and clean yourself energetically.

Each day you can find a few minutes to spare, so any protests about "I do not have time for this" are not true. Spend the next week giving yourself at least five minutes every evening to recapitulate your day. When you recapitulate daily, you will soon see how you gain energy to use for bigger cleaning projects. You will also strengthen your tracking skills.

People doing daily recapitulation often notice their dreams change. This is a sign of increased personal energy. Instead of spending your dreamtime to process your day, you clear your dreaming palate to taste other forms of dreaming.

This recapitulation can be done for ten to fifteen minutes or longer. When I worked with don Miguel, our community gathered together once a week for extended sessions of recapitulation. Working with a group is a powerful way to increase the energy and go deeper. If you have extra time and energy, you can always do an extended recapitulation. Picking a specific topic (my first relationship, my last job, my fear of spiders) guides and supports your work.

STEPS OF RECAPITULATION

1) **Set your intent** on why you want to create more energy in your life. Your intent can be broad: "I want extra energy to help me break down my old structures." Or your intent can be specific: "My intent is to recapitulate my energy so I release my jealousy around Marsha." Decide what you want to recapitulate in this session: Do you want to recapitulate a certain event or age, or are you simply going back to see where you lost energy today? Make this clear so you can stay focused.

2) **Connect your will** to a higher energy source—the sun or earth work well. Do this by imagining a cord between your

solar plexus and the sun or earth. You can also link to the four elements. This link will strengthen your practice.

3) Either sitting or lying comfortably, *let your mind go back* to the beginning of your day. See the circumstances, people, and places of your day as clearly as possible, without getting attached to the emotional aspects of each scene. Breathe back your energy from this scene-either by visualizing your energy returning to you or by feeling the energy coming into your body, or both. Make your breath audible-one great technique is to imagine yourself as a vacuum cleaner, inhaling your energy out of the scene.

Pay attention to what part of your body you feel the energy coming back to. Do not get caught in analyzing. Simply breathe in your energy. You can analyze and ponder later.

4) *Breathe out any energy you took* from someone else, or any agreements you made at the time. (Remember all this work is done with love, so if you begin to feel judgmental or angry, shift to recapitulating something that is not as painful emotionally.) Imagine breathing in your energy, and breathing back any energy you may have taken on that does not belong to you. If you feel that you sent out some negative energy in the past, you can practice breathing this in and then breathing it down to the earth beneath you, and letting the Earth transform this old energy.

5) You may find your mind jumping from image to image. *Keep breathing in your energy,* and let whatever pictures that come up be. You may need to bring yourself back

to the scene you initially set out to recapitulate if you find your mind is trying to drag you away from it.

6) Recapitulation can last briefly or for as long as you can stay focused. Keep remembering to *return your awareness* to your breath and your intent. The audible breath will help you stay focused. You can start from the beginning of your day and move to the present, start at the present and go backward through time to the beginning of your day, or let your mind reveal the places you lost the most energy during the day. If other events or circumstances present themselves as you recapitulate, feel free to either ignore them or recapitulate them.

7) When you feel complete, take three deep breaths, and visualize that you are using light to *clear out* anything that does not belong to you in this moment. Release your connection to the earth, sun, or the four elements. You may want to say a prayer of thanks.

Over time as you continue this practice you will feel an increase of energy in your body.

You can also do mini-recapitulation sessions during the day, anytime. Set your intent, call in the four elements, and consciously breathe back your energy.

To support your practice, you may wish to use my CD, *Returning to Center: Meditations and Recapitulation,* which thoroughly describes the recapitulation process and leads you through a fifteen-minute guided recapitulation. See the Resources section at the back of the book for more information.

THE ART OF SORTING

This exercise is a continuation of the mind exploration and tracking exercises discussed in the last chapter. You can use it in conjunction with recapitulation.

Continue witnessing and taking notes of your thoughts and experiences. Begin to sort: What are your short-term cleaning projects, and what are your long-term cleaning projects? Track your short-term projects to discern what the deeper structure might be.

If you have non-judgmental, clear friends who know you well, ask them to help you see any hidden agreements that may not be noticeable because of the cleverness of your gremlins.

You do not need to remember how you created the structure, but by keeping your awareness and watching your gremlins, you can begin to make educated guesses. Keep a log of what you find for at least a month, noting your perceptions and any information you get from friends. Then make very clear action steps for short-term cleaning. Have a second list of actions ready for when you have more energy to focus on long-term cleaning.

Keep your lists handy as a valuable resource to refer to when dirt arises, or when you feel ready to roll up your sleeves and scrub the deeper layers of dirt.

CONNECTING TO THE ELEMENT OF FIRE

Cleaning means letting go of the past and embracing the present moment. Here is a short practice for connecting the element of fire and the art of cleaning. It is especially potent after doing recapitulation.

Read through the gremlin tactics again. On five pieces of small paper, write down five ways you sabotage, distract, or limit yourself. Build a fire in your fireplace, make a bonfire outside, or put equal parts rubbing alcohol and epsom salts into a fireproofed container and light. It burns beautifully. Two layers of aluminum foil formed in a shallow bowl over an old pot works well for burning this mixture, or use a large metal container on bricks.

Hold your paper in your hand and close your eyes. Ask yourself if you are really ready to let go of these tactics. If you are, thank them out loud one by one. This honors that the gremlins' initial intent was to keep you safe, and lets them know you are now ready to live another way. For example, "Thank you for constantly projecting my fears that other people will not like me."

After you speak your word or sentence of thanks, say out loud, "I now release you to the fire of change" and put the paper into the fire. Feel the fire within consuming these old beliefs as you watch the fire turn the paper into ash.

Repeat as often as you like. By doing this practice, you will become adept at noticing what you want to release, thanking it, and then letting it go into the cleansing fire of your spirit.

INNeR ÇUIDANCe

FIRE VISUALIZATION FOR CREATING A NEW CONTAINER

Your second guardian is from the element of fire. From fire we learn the art of inner cleaning, the right use of action.

L et your body be comfortable and take some deep breaths into your belly. Imagine yourself standing in the middle of your beautiful stone circle. Face your symbol for the element of air and say hello. Turning to face another direction, ask for guidance and energy from the element of fire, to give yourself courage and strength to open the door of your closet.

Invite a fire guide to join you and support you in taking responsibility for cleaning your structure. Be open to how that guide may appear. Your fire guide may be an animal, a person you know, or a stranger. It may be a quiet voice in your head, or a knowing in your body. Your guardian of fire may not come to you immediately, but later in a dream or while you are in the middle of your day this guide may appear. Pray for the power to clean even the toughest dirt with grace and joy.

When you feel complete, ask for a symbol to represent this new anchor, and place it in one direction of your circle.

Place an object on your altar to represent fire and your new intent: a candle, a washcloth, or any object that pleases you. Ask to use all of the elements and their gifts wisely to guide you through cleaning your old structure and coming to center in your authentic self.

*You could not step twice into the same
river; for other waters are ever
flowing on to you.*

> *Heraclitus (540 BC - 480 BC),
> "On the Universe"*

*When one door of happiness closes,
another opens; but often we look so long
at the closed door that we do not see the
one which has been opened for us.*

> *Helen Keller (1880 - 1968)*

WATER

the art of opening

The gift of water is learning to open ourselves to all things. It is easy to stay open to things we like or that feel good, and more difficult to stay open to things we dislike or that feel bad. To open means accepting all that life brings while simultaneously choosing to act for positive change.

Opening is not a passive mood of discouraged acceptance towards your inner world or outer reality. It is a courageous internal movement of trust in the unfolding of life.

Many religions use water as a means to purify and open to spirit. Before entering the mosque to pray, Moslems respectfully wash their hands and feet. Christians are baptized as children or as adults to purify themselves and open to accept God. Many shamanic traditions use water to create sacred space before ceremony. When we align with the element of water, we connect with many practices of purification to prepare for something new.

Opening allows the opportunity for miracles to occur, and provides room for spirit to enter. It frees what is not longer useful and expands us beyond the known.

DISSOLVING WHAT IS STUCK

As you continue your journey of clearing your vision and cleaning your being, you will open many doors that lead to stuck emotions. By staying equally open to the "good" and the "bad" feelings, you create space to allow healing to dissolve your old structure. When you open the doors of your emotions, you allow cleansing waters to flow. Flowing water has huge power. It will dissolve what is stuck and unblock what is jammed within.

A great story about the power of water comes from a master of yoga, Yogi Bhajan. Imagine your unconscious as a dirty pan of oil. Whenever you do any healing work, it is as if you begin pouring pure, clear water into the pan of oil. What happens when water and oil come together? Since oil and water do not mix, the oil will start coming to the surface. The oil represents all of your old emotions and agreements. So as the water of clarity pours in, the difficult emotions rise to the surface (and become conscious). Can you remain open to everything that arises so it can overflow and be released?

Whenever you create more flow around your stagnant structure, long-forgotten emotions begin to float into your conscious mind. Your initial reaction may be to resist these old emotions. This resistance arises because, early on, you learned to shut down the uncomfortable parts of your conscious mind. You might think, "If I pretend my closet is already clean, maybe no one will notice," or "If I keep the door closed long enough, perhaps the gremlins and monsters will go away."

You may believe that if you close your senses down, if you keep all the taps of your emotions closed, you will stay safe. But imagine living in a house where all the drains are clogged with old sludge and you refuse to turn on the water for fear of what might overflow. Soon not only do you have the backlog of sludge but also overflowing toilets and of piles of unwashed clothes.

This tactic of keeping your emotions dammed up may have once worked to some extent. As a child it may have allowed you to survive in overwhelming emotional situations. As an adult closing down strengthens the rigid structures that limit you. The same responses that helped you survive the ups and downs of your childhood now keep you from being flexible and present as an adult.

For example, the thought "Mom loves my brother more than me" could become the belief that no one could ever really love you. Every time you are in a relationship and feel loved, that new energy would flow around your old "no one loves me" agreement. Getting the love you so desperately crave would be like pouring clear water into your being and stirring up all the mud of old emotions to come to the surface. Your fear of abandonment and loss would arise. Without awareness, you unconsciously create a drama to explain your emotions, and then blame your partner for your uncomfortable feelings.

The pattern of closing becomes so habitual it is hard to recognize. With practice you can learn to notice when you are closing, before you start making up stories and intensifying the emotions.

Here is a good way to begin to sense the difference in your being between staying open or closing. Shut your eyes and feel in your body a time you took something very personally, a time when you felt offended or angry or resentful of someone else's actions. It may be something that happened yesterday, or something that happened ten years ago. Visualize something that was very painful at the time. How did your body feel? Take a moment to experience the emotions and sensations in your body while you imagine something that hurt you.

Most of us feel a constriction, a tightening in our body, when we take something personally. There is a feeling of becoming smaller, of closing in. The mind perceives we are being judged or wronged in some way, and our old thoughts trigger our emotional body.

Now feel a time you could have taken something personally, but did not—perhaps something in the past that would have hurt you, but this particular time did not. How did your body feel? How did this feel different from when you took something personally? Notice if an image or symbol arises to show the difference between these two states of being.

When you do not take an event or confrontation personally, there is a sense of fluidity in the body. You keep your happiness and balance because you are open. Instead of feeling the grip and weight of your structure, you feel the space of your true being.

When you open, you allow old emotions to flow through you on their way out, rather than stagnating. Resisting old emotions only keeps out authentic healing. A stream blocked by debris will become stagnant. Removing dead leaves and trash allows for cleansing flow. Open the faucets and let the plumbing in your house function as it is meant to.

WHY RESISTANCE IS futile

Resisting, or wishing things were different, is a way we close around our pain. Another way is to compare ourselves with others. We cause most of our own suffering not because of the actual emotional pain, but because of our reaction to it.

As you release your need to control your emotions, you align with the natural flow of energy. When you do not resist your structure while simultaneously not believing in it, you reclaim strength from it.

Resistance stops the flow of energy. If the voice of the old structure is talking loudly, and your reaction is to try and fight it, the only thing that wins is the old structure, for it now has your undivided attention. Resistance is the opposite of opening. By staying aware, you can use your emotions as a way to uncover the underlying structure.

When I first starting working with don Miguel Ruiz and the Toltec community, my resistance was fierce. I prided myself on being tough and independent. The truth is, I was terrified of disapproval. I would often spend the first two days of a workshop struggling with enormous resistance to any new information. My structure was being threatened, and I felt like I was fighting with all my might to keep from drowning.

One of my big shifts happened when I stopped judging my own resistance and opened beyond what I knew. This happened gradually, culminating in an experience in Peru six or seven years ago. My dear friend and mentor Gini was determined to support me in moving beyond my need for self-importance. She hatched a plan with don Miguel to place me in silence where I could be in service and gratitude for the first part of the journey.

Shifting from being a teacher to being in silence was okay at first. I practiced paying attention to everything around me, and being open. That lasted for about one day. Then my structure started to assert itself. By day two, I was starting to see that I had things I wanted to share. I was important. I had a right to teach. "Why is Gini doing this to me? She is obviously trying to control me." I bounced from self-criticism to severe judgment to terror to resistance to anger. I was not being valued! I was being ignored! I wanted to fight for my rights! I knew there was a lesson in there somewhere, but my own resistance stopped me from seeing what it was.

One morning while we were still in Peru, Gini asked me to help her plan a ritual. Planning rituals is one of my favorite things to do, but at this moment I exploded angrily as if she had asked me to clean a hundred toilets. I think I cursed at Gini and ran out the door. I was furious. How dare she think she could make me be in silence for days on end and then ask me to create a ceremony! How dare she!

Looking back, my strong reaction now seems comical. But at the time, I was so pushed by my own need to be independent and important that I was blind. I knew that a spiritual person is not supposed to be in resistance, but there I was! I stormed out of the hotel and furiously walked into Machu Picchu. It was raining hard, but I decided to climb Waynu Picchu, a beautiful, sacred, and very steep mountain at the edge of the city.

My anger kept growing as I climbed the mountain. I could not decide if I should toss myself off the cliff for being such a miserable excuse of a spiritual being or go back and yell at Gini for mistreating me. The rain intensified and the stone steps became steeper and more slippery. I soon came to a point of choice. I knew I could hold onto my anger, or I could continue up the mountain. I did not have the energy to do both. As I took the next step, I opened to my anger. I surrendered. I stopped resisting my own resistance, and watched the emotions and struggle wash away with the rain as I continued to climb.

What caused me to resist being in silence was what Gini calls "a perceived threat to your image." My image was telling me, "If you were really important and a good girl, you would be teaching instead of being quiet and serving. If you were really spiritual, you would be okay with being in service. If you were special, you would get the lesson."

My point of choice was simple: to remain closed or to open. By a gift of grace (and pure exhaustion), I chose to open and keep moving on my path and up the mountain. I saw there was nothing to defend or fight against. As I climbed Waynu Picchu, my heart opened. I simply was. I did not need to be right. Everything melted. I stopped identifying with my old stories and let go of my need to be seen in any particular way.

When you fight against your stories, they gain energy. When I hear people say, "I am never, ever going to do that again!" I am fairly certain they will be doing just that in the near future. When you open and say, "Thank you, agreement, for the ways you have served me. I release you and choose to accept love," you take the power from the old structure and give it to the new.

When you open you become so much larger than your fears; they are like spider webs instead of barbed wire. But when you fight your own structure, you cut yourself on its sharp edges. As you surrender to the immense flow between the solidity of your structure you will soon tap into an ocean of new resources and options.

opening beyond fear

Fear traps you under the weight of your emotions. When you think the emotions will never end and you close down, you feel you are drowning and there is no way out. You grasp for something to hang onto, and your panic increases.

As you open to the flow of your emotions, you keep your eyes open. You learn to swim in the current—not to fight it, but to stay aware as it flows through you. You become an underwater explorer, a fish able to breathe water through your heart.

One day a student, who was in great fear at the time, called me on the phone. After years of numbness, Michael was starting to experience his emotions. The intensity of them scared him, and he was starting to shut back down again in an effort to make the pain stop. He imagined all of his emotions spilling out of an overflowing box and drowning him. Michael's impulse was to slam the lid back down and stop the flow.

I said to him "Instead of using the fear as a trigger to shut back down, can you keep a tiny crack open for love to enter? Your fear is a sign of transformation, not a warning to stop." Later, he told me he imagined putting the lid on his box loosely, and invited healing to enter into his pain. He still felt his emotions, but his awareness had expanded to hold the box and its contents in his hands. Michael found spaciousness for clearing his repressed emotions, and saw that the fear was actually telling him he was on the right track.

Your energetic structure is a living being. It is held together by your belief in it, and fed by your energy. You created it to help yourself feel safe and to make sense of the world around you. As you journey deeper into yourself, you start to weaken the old structure. Emotions get shaken up. And of course your body becomes fearful. Your disaster mind starts yelling, "Danger! Danger!" and triggers your emotions to bounce all over the place. This is normal.

When you hit tremendous fear within yourself, this is sometimes a signal that you are moving closer to the foundation. How wonderful! Do not use this fear to dissuade you from your task. Fear is energy. Move fear into excitement by accepting the fear and allowing it to flow into something new. Instead of saying to yourself, "I am afraid, I am afraid, I can't do this," start saying, "I am excited. I am willing to be uncomfortable. I am excited about transforming my fears into love by not judging myself."

Don Miguel taught me a wonderful lesson about jumping into the waters of your fear over and over again as a way of healing. In 1996, don Miguel came close to drowning during a journey to Palenque, Mexico. Two years later I went snorkling with him in Maui. We put a life vest on him and he eagerly jumped in the water, only to madly scramble out again. As he sat panting on the deck of the boat, I asked him what was wrong. "This is the first time I have been in the water since I almost drowned," he said, "and my body remembers the fear."

"Okay!" he said, and smiling at me he jumped back into the water.

I watched him jump in and get out of the water three or four times, each time with less panic. Soon he was paddling around in the water happily. Don Miguel modeled how to open to fear and move beyond it, by being willing to smile and then with awareness plunge in again and again until the fear diminished. He did not close down and say, "I should not feel this fear," or "The fear means I should not get in the water." His intent was to enjoy the water, and so he simply kept showing his body it was safe until it trusted again.

At the pivotal times in your life, remember the larger perspective of what you are doing. If you pay attention only to the fear, you will back off, and nothing will change. If you open to bigger sight, you will see the perfection of your terror, the rightness of being uncomfortable. You are actively dismantling the old and making room for the new. Keep jumping in with your heart open until the fear subsides.

staying open

There are times when you will see an old agreement, know how it is hurting you, and choose to continue your behavior. If you do this, do not judge yourself; stay open to the ramifications of that agreement in your life. Sometimes it is too scary to release the old behavior, or you still have something to learn from it. Stay open. Sometimes you do not quite have the energy to make the change. Be gentle with yourself. Keep your awareness and your heart open, and you will gradually take yourself into a new way of being.

Sometimes, our greatest awakenings happen in the most difficult situations. What is revealed during these times can be shocking. One of the best times to practice opening is when you are overwhelmed. Can you open to whatever is in the present moment? "Oh, now I feel terror in my body. I open to this terror and let it move through me." "Ah, I feel closed and numb and unavailable. It is okay to be closed."

I was in a romantic relationship awhile ago that was very painful. We seemed to bring out the worst in each other. I was miserable, trying to figure out: "What part of this dynamic is mine, what is his, and why is it so hellish?" Despite much love between us, the drama was intense. One week we battled yet again, and I prayed that I would do something different this time. I decided to go fully into the emotions that were coming up, to open to them. I let go of the places I was holding onto, such as, "He is making me feel this way, or I am bad for feeling this way," and slid into the current of emotion.

The emotions were as intense as before I let go, but I maintained my open awareness. I felt my pain very deeply as part of me stayed open and curious. When I came out the other side, I felt something I could not name had been cleaned and purified within me. I was better able to listen openly to my partner without judgment or fear.

Soon after this experience, I heard myself thinking, "I just want to be loved!" I stopped and opened to this thought: "I just want to be loved. I just want to be loved." Then I saw that if this was true, I would be loved.

I asked myself, "If you look openly at what you have created in this relationship, what do you really want?"

And the answer I heard was "To be punished because I am bad."

Now, that was not the answer I was expecting. I almost dismissed it as some random thought. But since I had so recently witnessed myself go through intense emotional upheaval, I paid attention. At that point, it was not important for me to figure out where I took on an agreement as strange as "I need to be punished." The source was not important, but what I was doing with it was. Did I really want to be punished? Was that my deepest truth?

The truth was I usually felt a low level of guilt and therefore needed to be punished. When I looked at my relationship, I realized that this was clearly being reflected back to me. If I wanted to be loved unconditionally, I would have been loved unconditionally. But since I wanted to be punished, I was getting emotionally beaten up. It was a perfect setup. I was getting exactly what some part of me was asking for. Strange, but true.

As I opened to clarity, the muck of my old agreements arose into my conscious mind, and I could then make a conscious choice. When I saw this agreement, I did not make it anybody's fault. I did not spend a lot of time trying to figure out where it came from. Instead I just said to myself, "I don't want that anymore. I'm done. I am ready to release it." Eventually this caused it to dissolve, since I had opened to no longer believing the old agreement. The clear water of opening to acknowledge this agreement allowed the oil it had created to float up and out.

from the divine to the screaming child

The gift of opening to change in your life allows you to move smoothly through transitions from an old structure to a new one, while maintaining your center. You are willing to see what you are doing and to take responsibility for your actions, no matter what they are. You learn to accept and love all aspects of yourself, from the divine to the screaming child. Each emotion, and each reaction, teaches you something new; it offers you another pearl when you keep your eyes and heart open.

Here are some tips to facilitate your process of opening.

PATIENCE

Opening is a gradual process. You do not wake up one day and say, "Hey, I think I'll open to this immense pain I am in." It takes practice and persistence. The truth is that each of us knows how to open. We do this naturally when we feel safe. We can also learn to open when we do not feel safe or when we feel challenged in some way.

FIND THE SOURCE

As you increase your openness, you begin to see that most of your emotional reactions are not about the present at all.

Keep opening the doors into the past, and you will often track the real source of your pain. Seek out the scared child, the lonely teenager. What agreements might they have made?

EMBRACING

When you find a frightened and confused part of yourself, embrace it with open arms. Intimacy is showing up for yourself, whether you are feeling on top of the world or terrified. Make space for all of your emotional self.

HEALING

Sometimes you search for and find agreements that are causing your suffering. Other times you do not need to search, but only to make space for the shift to occur. Opening itself is all that is needed to release the old. Your disaster mind might be yelling and screaming the entire time, your body may be in fear, and the healing will still occur. Stay open to the possibility of being a tiny bit more open than before.

DAILY PRACTICE

Like clear perception and active cleaning, opening is best practiced daily. What is important is not the amount you open, but the consistent thread of teaching yourself to open as an automatic response. It is the effort, not the immediate result, that matters.

GRATITUDE

When you go into gratitude, you open. When you think of someone you love, you open. When you see a baby, or a puppy, you open. Study this sensation in your body. What does it feel like when you open? What causes you to open? What causes you to close down?

STRETCHING

In this moment, what can you do to open just a little bit more? Try shifting your posture or taking a deep breath, or thinking of a specific color filling your body. Does a particular movement or color or thought help you to open? Each moment, notice and play with what will open you just a tiny bit more. Focus only on the present moment. You will notice that an easy way to close down is to think of the future, or to compare yourself with someone else. Your journey to opening lies in this moment. Be where you are, and open to this moment with compassion.

ALLOWING PURE EMOTIONS

You may also begin to experience pure emotions, separate from any story or belief. After the end of one relationship, I spent a year watching my guilt. I started by noticing when I felt guilty and tracking it to an immediate source. Then I started tracking it back to a possible past source. In the end I realized I had always felt guilty. Period. There was no way I was acting to create guilt in my life, or anything looming from my past to account for it. I could invent all sorts of stories to find a way for the guilt to make sense, but they were simply that—stories. The truth is, we live in a very guilt-ridden culture. I absorbed it. Period. Recognizing that it was not mine, I could open to it and let it go. When it arose, I could say, "Oh, look, it is guilt," and open to releasing it. If I had continued to clamp down on the guilt, what do you think would have happened?

Progress does not mean not having emotions. Being centered is accepting and opening to whatever emotions are present. Deeper and deeper levels will continue to emerge. As the trapdoors open wide and unconscious agreements surface, more cleaning occurs. Be aware that the deeper you go, the more intense the feelings may become. This is not a failure, but a blessing. The question is, are you willing to release and open to something greater? Can you find excitement even in the discomfort of your familiar structure dissolving?

As you continue to open, self-discovery and learning becomes a joy. You move from resistance and fear to pouring more water into your being, becoming openly curious about what will come up next.

Fear and the many emotions that stem from fear—such as anger, justification, and resistance—will arise and fall. Like the flow of water, none of these emotions is permanent. Allow them to move naturally through you.

When we open and release our old emotions by being willing to simply witness them, our emotional body is able to function as it is supposed to. Then new emotions do not stick, but move through quickly and cleanly. A healed emotional body is a source of information and a vital connection to our intuition.

pRactices

INVESTIGATING CLOSING

Write down five things that cause you to close. For example:

My boss when she gets angry
The thought of war
When I feel jealous
When I fear I am going to be abandoned
When I take responsibility for other people's emotions

Take a couple of minutes for each of these five things, and write down exactly what it is that causes you to close: What is the core, the foundational image or emotion, that makes you close down?

example

My boss when she gets angry

I hate people getting angry at me. It makes me feel small and out of control. I feel helpless, the way I felt when I was a child and my mom yelled at me. I want her to love me, and I believe she doesn't. I want to defend myself, to make her wrong.

Emotionally, keep investigating why you would need to close down when your boss gets angry. It is not her anger that causes you to close, but some reaction inside of you from the past.

Pick one of these reactions and practice opening to it a little bit each day. Carefully watch the thoughts and emotions that arise as you practice opening. These thoughts will show you the structure that keeps you closed. Clean out what is not yours by doing recapitulation, or by imagining a sparkling stream running through your emotional body until it opens all the clogged and muddy channels.

opening to new possibilities

Often we close down because our disaster mind is telling us a story based on past events, we believe the story, and it triggers an old emotional response. Each time you notice disaster mind telling you a story that causes you to close or you feel your emotional body going into an old fear, make up three different possible stories that help you open. The more outrageous these stories are the better.

Making up new stories moves the emotions in your body, and will sometimes completely shift the dynamic. In any case, it will shift your response to the disaster mind-emotional reaction pattern, which is the most important thing.

Sometimes the stories will come in hindsight. Write them down. Eventually you will be able to make up stories in the present moment. This is a great way to break up your rigid thinking and structures, and create more space. The more humor you can bring to this process, the better.

exampLe	diaster mind's story	emotionaL response
I close down when my boss yells at me.	"You are in trouble, you are going to get fired, no one likes you, you must defend yourself or you will be run over ..."	Fear, panic, desire to run from the situation

possibLe new stories	new emotionaL response
My boss likes yelling as a way to communicate. I can respect that and open to listening.	Curiosity
My boss is an alien who thinks all human beings communicate through yelling.	Humor-acceptance
I am open to being yelled at because I know she cares about me deeply.	Acceptance

So what if these new stories are not true? The emotions stirred up by your disaster mind are not based in reality either! Use this exercise to have some fun and get out of a stuck pattern at the same time.

connecting to the element of water

When I am focusing on staying open and letting old emotions come to the surface I will sometimes take as many as three baths a day. Immersing myself in water calms my emotional body and reminds me of the nature of fluidity. Do not hesitate to use the element of water extensively as you work with your emotional body.

To connect with the element of water, consciously prepare a bath for yourself. Use epsom salts and essential oils. As you soak in the bath, imagine the water seeping into you and dissolving your old structure or any stuck emotions. Let yourself be held by the water, and allow the water to open you. Accept all of your emotions, let them flow, and then invite the water to wash them away. When you feel complete, pull the plug and visualize letting everything go down the drain.

You can do a mini-version of this practice by consciously connecting to water every time you wash your hands, and reminding yourself about the power of accepting the flow of life.

inner guidance

WATER VISUALIZATION FOR CREATING A NEW CONTAINER

Your third guardian is the element of water. From water you learn the art of opening, the right use of your emotional flow.

Let your body be comfortable, and take some deep breaths into your belly. Imagine yourself standing in the middle of your beautiful stone circle. Greet your symbols for the elements of air and fire. Turning to face a new direction, ask for guidance and energy from the element of water, to give you the willingness and faith to surrender to what is.

Invite a water guide to join you and support you in releasing your resistance and contraction. Be open to how that guide may appear. Your water guide may be an animal, a person you know, or a stranger. It may be a quiet voice in your head, or a knowing in your body. Your guardian of water may not come to you immediately, but later in a dream or while you are in the middle of your day. Water may show its many forms to you. Pray for the grace to open and expand in difficult times.

When you feel complete, ask for a symbol to represent this new anchor, and place it in one direction of your circle.

For your altar, pick an object to represent water and place it in one of the directions on the outside of the circle. You can represent water with a bowl of water, a statue of a dolphin, or any object that pleases you. Set your intent to use all of the elements and their gifts to guide you through the places you close down, riding the flow of your emotions to your center.

In Europe, the original tarot was a map to embodying the elements. Still popular today, each tarot card is an illustrated representation of ancient oral wisdom. The four suites of the tarot are based in the four elements: swords (air), wands (fire), cups (water), and disks (earth). The elements are also related to a different part of self: mind (air), energy (fire), emotional (water) and physical (earth). The tarot represents the journey we each take though different archetypes and elements to reclaim our full, authentic self.

We must learn not to disassociate the airy flower from the earthy root, for the flower that is cut off from its root fades, and its seeds are barren; whereas the root, secure in Mother Earth, can produce flower after flower and bring their fruit to maturity.

Kabbalah

If you can't feed a hundred people, then feed just one.

Mother Teresa (1910 - 1997)

EARTH

the art of nourishing

The final element in our circle is earth. Earth represents our physical body, and the need to nourish ourselves from the inside out. Opening allows us to delve into and clean the darker aspects of our being; the earth's nourishing aspects feed our center so it shines brightly.

The foundations of your life are based on false beliefs you made as a child or agreements that were passed down to you. As the structure built on this faulty base begins to crack apart, the temptation is to buttress it and reinforce it with duct tape. If you let the old foundation fall apart, you feel there will be nothing to hold you steady. But underneath this false foundation is the true solidity of your being.

The fourth element teaches you to send your roots to your true soil.

My favorite analogy for this concept comes from farming. Conventional farming focuses on keeping pests and diseases away from crops, using pesticides and herbicides. The result is toxic plants and soil that is slowly poisoned. Fertilizers are then used on the depleted soil to give the plants what they need to grow.

Organic farming focuses on keeping the soil and crops healthy. Organic farmers know that strong, healthy plants resist pests and diseases. The result is an emphasis on feeding the soil. Since each plant has different nutritional requirements, the soil is constantly tested and supplemented.

If you treat yourself the way conventional farmers treat their crops, you act to defend yourself from outside invaders. You use judgment, criticism, and comparison as your weapons. In the process, your own soil becomes toxic. You falsely believe you nourish yourself by keeping out what you do not like.

If you treat yourself the way organic farmers treat their crops, you keep your attention within, and focus on your own soil. You constantly ask, "What do I need to nourish myself in this moment?" Instead of fighting or trying to change the outside world, you strengthen the inner foundation.

NOURISHING YOUR OWN SOIL

How do you learn to nourish your own soil when so many weedlike thoughts and fears are clamoring for attention?

How do you get beneath the shell of your false foundation, which demands the toxicity of judgment to hold it together? What really nourishes your base?

Nourishment is the culmination of the earlier gifts of air, fire, and water. With air's clear perception, you learn to see your true needs rather than your surface structure. Fire's cleaning uncovers the neglected places and makes space for new agreements. Water's opening increases your self-intimacy and informs you where you need nourishing.

After cleaning and opening, nourishment is what you put into the space you have created. Nourishing is an art, a response to your deepest longing. Beneath the voices of the mind and your fearful emotions, a whisper of authentic need echoes. The structure yells to you, "I need to feel safe. I need to be protected. I need your attention." The shaky foundation beneath it claims it must be bolstered to keep everything in your life sane.

Your authentic foundation—your root system—whispers, "Look deeper. You are safe. The love is within." True nourishment helps you to support and strengthen this presence.

Nourishing yourself includes a willingness to discover what feeds your authenticity. You learn to nourish your roots by using your outer and inner life to guide you. The result is a new structure rooted in love and acceptance. From this sacred soil you can truly extend your roots and grow.

Like your other new tools of perception, cleaning, and opening, nourishing takes practice and experimentation. There are seeds of love and seeds of fear within you. What you nourish will grow. To flourish, your being requires unconditional and consistent care. The soil of your inner self needs to be watered and fed. Sporadic attention, flooding and then drought, or giving too many of your nutrients to others all weaken your core and stunt your development.

True nourishment comes drop by drop. Choosing to shift your perception is an act of nourishment. Cleaning out a reaction based on fear is an act of nourishment. Opening just that little bit more is an act of nourishment.

CRAVINGS AND NEEDS OF THE BODY

Care is needed to discern the blurry boundary between nourishing your true self and nourishing your false structure. Sometimes what feels truly nourishing in the moment is toxic in the long run, and what feels uncomfortable or even frightening in the short-term is deeply nourishing in the long-term.

When you begin to conceptualize your life as a process of long-term nourishment instead of short-term pleasure, the choices are easier.

An easy way to see this dynamic is with food. Many foods feel great in the short run, but in the long run can be very destructive. You may crave toxic foods, such as sugar and caffeine, even if they are hurting you. Only when you go beneath their addictive nature do you feel what your body really wants, which is healthy, sustaining food.

It is confusing when you crave toxic foods, and the same goes for toxic thoughts and actions. Conscious awareness teaches you what your true cravings are. When you are unconscious, you act in the short-term, for the immediate fix. As you nourish your awareness, you will begin to see the ramifications of your actions. You gain valuable information as you listen to the body as a guide and watch what you create in your life, always with an eye toward long-term, sustainable nourishment.

As part of this process, when you eat any type of food, whether it is physical, emotional, or mental, you learn to ask yourself, "What is this nourishing?" "Is this food creating fear or joy?" "Is this toxic, or sustaining?" Simple witnessing teaches you what you are nourishing, and gives you the opportunity to shift. Remember you may witness the toxic effects of a behavior for a while before you have the energy to shift it. Be patient and allow yourself the space without judgment to make the change.

Openly listen to your impulses. Do they take you toward acceptance and joy, or toward fear and contraction? As you explore, you will learn to distinguish the impulses of long-term nourishment versus short-term relief.

Imagine yourself as a plant ready to flower. Start by honoring your roots. For humans, the roots are your simple bodily needs: good sleep, good food, exercise, loving touch. Make sure you start here. Pay attention to how much sleep your body needs. Take note of how different foods shift your moods and sense of physical well-being. Getting clear on these basics will solidify your new foundation.

How you care for your body affects your emotions, energy, and perception. You may notice many things you want to change about your basic habits. Do not try and make too many changes at once. Pick a few to focus on, create the change, and move on to the next. Do not sabotage yourself by taking on so much you become overwhelmed. Nourishing is a gradual, moment-by-moment process. Like cleansing, nourishing is not something that is done just once.

DURING a CRISIS

Remembering how to nourish yourself in the middle of an emotional crisis is tricky. When you feel good, it is easier to recognize what is sustaining and what is toxic. But when you get caught in an old emotion, when you feel scared or out of control or insecure, you revert back to toxic thoughts and behaviors. You judge and compare yourself. Or you see yourself as a helpless victim without any power. Or you stop taking responsibility for yourself. You plunge into disaster mind, and project your fears onto others. These behaviors encourage your old structure, but starve your inner being.

It takes great awareness to see your behaviors, and even greater courage and energy to change them. This change comes from learning to nourish yourself in spite of, and through, your fear and judgment. Compassion, patience, humor, and trust are needed. When you feel that you are falling on your face, expressing these qualities to yourself is difficult, but crucial. Nourish yourself through all phases of the healing cycle.

I recently heard a great story about choosing to nourish oneself despite an embarrassing situation. My friend Maria one day filled her diesel truck with unleaded gasoline. "Usually, I would have judged myself horribly. Instead I noticed my mistake, called a friend to come help me out, and waited. My mind stayed clear, and I spent the time stretching and breathing, helping myself get more present. It was exciting to make a mistake and realize I could still be good to myself!"

Just the way water soaks into the earth, our intent to nurture ourselves soaks into our being. Our minds may tell us, "Nothing is growing, nothing is changing, this is hopeless," but our bodies are soaking in new nutrients. Eventually the seeds of love will manifest in our lives. Each tiny act of compassion, or forgiveness, or joy, even if we do not feel it in the moment, soaks through the web of our structure and activates our new foundation.

BReakiNG HaBitual patteRNS

The process works best when you remain aware and continually clear out what no longer sustains you. Something that nourished you in the past may one day be toxic. Something that appears toxic may be vitally nourishing. Be willing to investigate, to ask questions, to watch, and to wait.

I remember a time my body loved sugar. I was working the night shift at a newspaper, and I consumed a great deal of sugar and caffeine to keep me going. I was young and wired and could go for days with little sleep. I was physically healthy, rarely sick, and excited about my life.

One day I experienced a drastic shift. After ten years of drinking sugary iced tea with impunity, I started to feel lethargic and sick. I soon noticed a relationship between my level of sugar consumption and not feeling well. When I really paid attention to my body, I realized I had to stop eating sugar. I fought this realization for a while. How could this be possible? I'd always eaten sugar. But for two years if I ate a bite of pie or took a sip of any sugary drink, my body reacted violently. Something that had once felt very nourishing to me was now toxic. For a long time I still craved sugar. Eventually this shifted. As my body healed, it stopped yearning for sugar.

Similarly, you can track and learn what is nourishing to you and what is not. You may find patterns and behaviors that were once nourishing to you but now weaken you. Something that others say is nourishing may not be what you need in the moment. Keep your long-term vision focused on your greater intent as you make new choices in the moment.

Sometimes nurturing yourself is doing exactly the opposite of what your habitual reaction would be. Such acts will not feel completely comfortable in the moment, but they are long-term nourishment. If you are a perfectionist, a nourishing act might be to allow yourself to make mistakes and celebrate them. If you are afraid to make choices, a nourishing act might be to make a definite decision and follow through on it each day. If you are anxious, a nourishing act might be to focus on your breath every five minutes. If you are used to doing everything by yourself, asking a friend to simply hold you might be nourishing. If you always rely on others to make you feel better, spending time alone might be nourishing.

Sometimes a simple act of nourishment will reveal deep hungers and pain. As you begin to nourish yourself, you may discover that a huge part of your structure is, for example, based on believing you do not deserve love. When you start feeding a part of yourself that has been starved and cut off, the hunger can seem more intense. Reassure yourself that you will not abandon yourself again, and that you will nurture and support yourself.

feeding the frozen aspects of yourself

I spent years trying to ignore and think my way out of the fear, sense of scarcity, and grief in my body. All my nourishing energy went toward figuring out how I could make my difficult feelings go away. I nurtured ways to avoid pain and ignore the terror that would creep in. I believed, "If only I could run faster than this it will go away. I would be okay, if only the fear would leave me alone."

Slowly, I learned to stop running away; I learned to become still and go into my body rather than ignoring it. This was difficult.

I recognized my level of self-abandonment when I did yoga by myself for the first time. As I held the first pose, I wept for no apparent reason. My body was terrified and confused, and also relieved that I was bringing my attention to it.

One of the main reasons we have lost the art of nourishing ourselves is our desire to hide from old pain. Each of us has a child trapped within our structure, frozen in time. Most of our emotional reactions in the present are the reactions of this child, not the adult. Cleaning and opening reveal these old patterns and reactions and the immense emotional energy they carry. Nourishing heals these places.

Your structure is held in place by the energy of old stuck agreements and stories from your past. When you open to all of your being, you embrace the frightened child, the gawky teenager, and the angry toddler. Instead of ignoring the frightened child, or wishing the gawky teenager would go away, you can nourish each aspect of yourself. Just as you learn to nourish yourself in the moment at each part of the cycle, you also learn to nourish all of your various ages.

What does the frightened child need from you? How can you reassure the gawky teenager? Can you make space for the angry toddler to discover what lies beneath the anger?

Befriending the body is one of your greatest sources of power. To truly befriend and nourish the body, you need two skills: the skill of listening with unconditional love, and the skill of creating appropriate boundaries.

Listening with unconditional Love

Our bodies store all of our old agreements. The crucial thing to remember is that the agreements you discover in your body—the fears, the paralysis, the insecurities—are coming from a child. The only way to shift this part of the structure is to listen to and nourish your child. You do not need to know exactly what the agreement was, but you do need to honor and create safe space for the child.

The adult part of you may think, "That is ridiculous. I can't believe that agreement!" Remember the child made the agreement with a child's mind. Sometimes these agreements are made even before you can speak. They are body memories and fears, not mere mental constructs.

When you listen, when you open wide, you become larger than the child and step into the role of nurturing parent. When you ask your child, "What do you need?" you begin the journey of nourishing the child into growing up.

Often the act of nourishing is as simple as choosing to stay home one evening, but often our resistance to honoring the child is huge. When we do not listen, the child either goes numb and silent, or increases the intensity of the feeling, until we forget our adult self and become the child.

When you cut off the child, you also cut off your creativity and joy. And no matter how hard you try to keep the child silent, eventually your child will emerge strongly. Something triggers an old memory, and suddenly you are taken over by huge emotions, body memories, and fears. You then begin reacting to the world around you from the hurt child's point of view. As you have probably seen, living from the hurt child's perspective creates chaos as the child tries to keep itself safe and get its needs met in an adult world.

If something feels uncomfortable, nourish yourself through it. Gently nudge yourself forward, rather than forcing yourself. Saying, "Let's sit with this uncomfortable place just a little bit longer" will allow you to keep your awareness as you delve into hard places within.

Nourishing is about honoring all parts of self. You can be a successful, respected businessperson and a grief-stricken three-year-old. You can be on a spiritual journey and be having two-year-old tantrums inside. One does not negate the other. Your deepest foundation holds all of you.

All your parts create who you are. You are a multi-dimensional being with complementary as well as contradictory emotions and beliefs occurring on different levels at the same time. The rebellious ten-year-old in you may inspire you to create art that no one has seen before, yet also cause you to be irresponsible and difficult in relationships. The six-year-old you who was the apple of your father's eye until you got buckteeth and he began to make fun of you, now desperately wants a man to love you as you are. Yet no other person, or anything else outside of you for that matter, can take away the pain. Although the adult in you knows the reality of relationships and can discern when a man is loving, to the six-year-old, every man is a disappointment.

I have learned to listen and slow things down when the child starts speaking. This does not mean that everything in my life comes to a halt, but that I open wider. I stretch. I expand, so I can be parent and child, so I can love and be loved, while continuing my life.

My clue that my child needs attention is a strong bodily sensation, or a loud, fearful mind. I usually go for a walk and ask myself, "What do you need?" The child has learned she can trust me, so she talks to me pretty quickly now. "I need to be held." And I will imagine holding her, sending her love. Sometimes she says, "I want you to stop taking that risk; it scares me." And with love I will tell her, "This is very important to me. I know it is scary, but I am right here with you."

This interchange often happens around my relationships. Often my child does not like it when I get more open or vulnerable with someone, and she will let me know. "We are going to get hurt!" I remind her that I am always with her, and that nothing can hurt her when I am around.

The biggest place of pain you carry is when you abandon yourself. Nourishing is about showing up for yourself, no matter what. Others may abandon you, betray you, hate you. This is a painful truth about life. But the greatest pain comes when you abandon, betray, or hate yourself. The greatest healing comes when you reclaim, nourish, and honor yourself, exactly as you are. Part of this healing comes from learning to make appropriate boundaries for yourself, and your child.

BOUNDARIES as NOURISHMENT

Creating a new structure entails building a safe container where you can heal old pain. Opening does not mean letting go of all boundaries. In fact, boundaries are a vital part of nourishing. One of the biggest gifts of the element of earth is clear boundaries. Most boundaries are limitations based on fear, and are used to defend a position. Boundaries made out of love and concern for your own growth and wholeness help keep you open.

Creating nourishing boundaries gives you a container to open and explore what lies within. You can make boundaries out of fear, to keep out experiences and emotions you do not like, but this action does not nourish you; rather, it causes you to close down and keep everything out, both good and frightening. When you make boundaries out of self-respect and honor where you are in the moment, you can stay open and allow nourishment to enter.

A very simple practice for setting a boundary is to take time for yourself. If you are serious about your return to center, you should be alone with yourself on a regular basis. Being in nature once a week, sitting quietly in the mornings, or taking yourself out to walk under the stars once a month are all ways of being with yourself. Carve out and nourish your time to look within, to become more intimate with yourself.

Do not use this time to judge or criticize yourself, no matter how bad you are feeling. Be with your child, or your gawky teenager. Ask them what they want, and nourish their deepest needs, beneath the fear and reaction. Notice the urge to hold your old, cracking foundation together. Practice sitting with the feeling and being uncomfortable in your body while you nourish yourself.

Making a safe container for the child does not mean giving your child everything he or she wants. Children need boundaries that arise out of love. Imagine if your child said, "I am going to eat the whole chocolate cake!" How would you make an appropriate boundary? Sometimes your child wants to do things that are not nourishing. Learn to set clear, loving boundaries.

You can learn to set internal, loving boundaries with the hurt child, so you do not continue the external cycle of drama and blaming others. It rarely helps to throw your pain unconsciously onto someone else, even though it might feel great in the moment. It is a short-term fix, but may be necessary when you first get in touch with the child. Move toward expressing the emotion first in a safe way, and then sharing later.

You might say to your child, "Yes, honey, I know that you want to scream and hurt those people who seem to be hurting you. Let's go for a long walk first and throw rocks at the water, and talk to them later." Or "Yes, it looks like those people really meant to hurt you. But they are just in pain themselves; it is not about us. Let's go take a bath and cry out some of this old pain and fear."

Creating a container means noticing your surroundings and choosing a safe place to express what is inside. You cannot always express what is inside you at any given moment. You may have an incident at work where you get emotionally triggered by something and feel a welling up of old pain. If you want the child to trust you, follow through and create a safe space at a later time. Trust builds from authentic listening and appropriate action. You can say to yourself, "I know this hurts, and we will make a safe space to cry later."

Trust also grows when you set appropriate external boundaries. It is an art to learn to say no with an open heart and a soft belly. It may take a while to build up to creating a firm yet open-hearted boundary.

Imagine you need to set a boundary with someone: a coworker who constantly interrupts you at your job. For days you have sent her subtle clues that you do not want to be interrupted. You have ignored her, invited her to talk with you after work, gossiped to others in your office about how this person is driving you crazy. The only thing left is to tell her not to interrupt you.

There are many different ways you can set this boundary. You can postpone setting the boundary for a long time and then blow up at her. You can get angry with her and shut your door whenever you see her coming. You can get someone else to tell her to stop interrupting you. You can tell her the boss is getting upset at you for not finishing your work on time.

Notice how setting these types of boundaries feels in your body. How does it feel when you do not tell others what you need, but instead hope they figure it out? How does it feel when you judge and become angry at them, and simply shut them out of your life? How does it feel when you blame someone else because you need things to be different?

These methods might work, but they cause you to close down. They do not teach you to speak your truth.

Learning to set boundaries without rejecting or projecting onto others, or needing them to be any different than they are, takes time. One approach is to practice in small doses. Imagine setting a boundary with the interrupting coworker while keeping yourself open and present. How would this look and feel?

You may be afraid to set boundaries for fear of hurting or upsetting others. This is short-term thinking. Not setting a simple boundary may feel easier in the moment, but the long-term ramifications are vast. One result is that you stop trusting yourself. The message you are giving your body is: "Your needs are not important."

Create boundaries to nourish yourself, rather than to make others behave a certain way. Boundaries are not for controlling others. "I want you to stop that behavior; it hurts me!" is not a boundary, but a demand. "I feel hurt when you get angry" implies their anger is hurting you. The truth is their anger is their anger, and your hurt is your hurt. Let them be angry, be open to your own hurt, and consciously choose your reaction. This is easier said than done, for in the heat of the moment you may react rather than choose. Again, move toward staying open and nourishing yourself, no matter what others are doing.

Making clear boundaries is about taking responsibility for yourself and your needs. Boundaries help you prevent taking on the problems of others.

You may not like what your current boundaries are. Your child may say, "I really need not to be sexual for awhile." Your adult may not like that idea. You can try negotiating and asking the child what it really needs. You may find that you need to honor what the child is asking for, and that you are willing to set that boundary, even though you are afraid about what your partner will say. At other times you may learn that you are not as open as you want to be, and that you still have rigid, fear-based boundaries about certain issues. Notice that you are a work in progress, and honor the current moment. Stretch yourself, but honor your limitations and boundaries.

It can be frightening to set boundaries. When you first start setting them, pay attention to what arises. Guilt, fear of rejection, shame, or insecurity may all arise to haunt you. Do not nourish these emotions; instead nourish the strength of your being that is beneath them. Know they are passing; they are from an old time.

Your goal is to move away from nourishing your old structure and toward nurturing your authentic center. Do not be surprised if a simple act of nourishing yourself or setting a boundary brings up big emotions. Remember, you are taking energy away from your old foundation and placing it into a new foundation. The old structure may fight and scream and try in a myriad of ways to hook your attention. Keep going back to your intent, and your four new foundational anchors connected with the four elements. Remind yourself that you are creating a new foundation to build a conscious house for yourself with much more room for your spirit.

Use the energy of your old foundation to nourish your new one. As you remove your attachment to the old structures, you free up energy. You can then take this energy and compost it into the soil of your being. There is no fight here, only the intent to allow the rigid and painful parts of your structure to dissolve into fertile compost for new growth.

pRactices

GROUNDING

It is very nourishing to connect your physical body to the earth through a process called grounding. Grounding settles and energizes you. It helps you release nervous or stuck energy and allows you to feel the strength and ease that comes from being supported unconditionally.

To ground yourself, sit comfortably. Breathe your awareness down into the base of your spine. Let your belly be soft. Imagine yourself as a tree, with roots that go deep into the earth and branches that stretch up to the sky. Let your spine form roots that spread out into the soil. Your branches reach up from the crown of your head and into the sky. Feel how your physical body, the trunk of your tree, rests perfectly between your roots and branches.

Imagine you can breathe energy and vitality through your roots up into your body. Breathe this energy all the way through your body, and send it out through your branches to the sky. Now imagine breathing the openness and vastness of space into your branches. Breathe this energy through your body and down into the earth.

With each breath, allow yourself to be held and support-ed by earth and sky. Feel the unlimited amount of energy available to you. Allow this energy to saturate into every cell of your body and create a sense of wholeness and connection. Let your mind be quiet, and let your body relax.

When you are finished, take three deep breaths into your heart and gently release your image of roots and branches.

I recommend doing grounding every day, along with doing your daily recapitulation. To support your practice, you may wish to use my CD, *Returning to Center: Meditations and Recapitulation,* which thoroughly describes the grounding process and leads you through a ten-minute guided grounding exercise. See the Resources section in the back of the book for more information.

As part of your grounding practice, also set aside a little time each day to listen to your body. Go for a slow walk in nature, do yoga, or simply sit quietly and tune in. Tell your body you are willing to listen and hear what it has to tell you. Invite your body to speak and share its fears and its wisdom.

Often our bodies will keep amplifying their messages until we hear them, or they stop talking to us at all. When you first begin to slow down and listen to your body, it may refuse to speak, or only yell at you for not paying attention. Be patient with yourself. Your body holds tremendous knowledge. Let it know you are willing to spend time nourishing its deepest needs. When you get a message, image, or feeling from your body, honor it while delving into the core of your truth. It may take time to re-establish a relationship with your body. Be patient and stay present with yourself.

tools for nourishing

Write down ten acts that nourish you. Here are some examples:

Playing with my dog
Hugging someone
Doing yoga
Taking a long walk
Reading spiritual books
Being in silence
Performing a ritual
Taking a hot bath
Watching children play
Dancing

Write your ten nourishing acts down on separate index cards. You can also draw them, or make ten mini-collages with photographs and magazine pictures.

Start by picking one of your cards each day and doing the action it suggests. Pay attention to how it nourishes you, and what you feel. This will give you a template to draw on later.

When you have completed all ten cards, begin to use these cards to explore opening yourself to more nourishment. Think of something that causes you to close down—a memory of your ex-husband or ex-wife, a fear of something in the future, or a situation at home. Pick one of the cards and focus on it. Weave the two feelings together; for example, take a hot bath while thinking about your ex. Relax into the practices and feelings that open you, and create a little bit more opening in your body for the situations and feelings that cause you to close down. What if you stayed open to a stressful situation and nourished yourself? What would the outcome be?

Start with small occurrences and build your way up to larger events.

When you are in crisis and want to nourish yourself, pick one of your cards. Put the card into action, either by doing it or meditating on what it feels like when you do it. Let it seep into your body. When you have the most resistance to using the card is the best time to take action! Keep inviting yourself to open and be nourished, even if the opening is only a tiny crack at first.

connecting to the element of earth

The act of nourishing a plant is a great way to connect with the element of earth in your everyday life. To learn about the cycle of growth, nurture a plant from a seedling until it is fully grown.

Planting seeds is best done in the spring or early summer, though it will work any time of the year with enough light and warmth. If you travel a lot, you can use a plant that doesn't need much water as your connection to earth.

Get a cup or planter box, and buy some seeds (tomatoes or sunflowers work well.) You can also buy a little herb garden starter kit in many garden stores.

When you plant the seeds, set an intent for what you want to nourish in your own life.

Examples:

"With this seed I set my intent to nourish my desire to have more friendship in my life."

"Just as I commit to taking care of this plant, I commit to taking care of my own need for good food and water."

"May I nourish the soul of my being just as I nourish this seedling."

Now plant your seeds or repot a plant: get your hands in the soil! You may want to write your intent and place it on or nearby the container. Each time you water, touch the soil and ask for a blessing on your own soil. Giving your new plant the consistent care it needs will remind you that your physical self needs the same attention and love. You will learn a lot about yourself and the process of growth as you nourish your plant.

As your plant gets bigger, you may need to repot it or find a good place to plant it outside. Always feel free to start over if something happens to your plant. Make it a practice until you have come to know intimately the nourishing power of earth.

> *The Native American sweat lodge is one of the most*
> *important traditions that embraces the elements. The*
> *lodge brings all four of the elements together as a ritual*
> *for physical and spiritual purification: water is poured*
> *over fire-heated rocks (earth) to create steam (air).*

INNER GUIDANCE

EARTH VISUALIZATION FOR CREATING A NEW CONTAINER

Your fourth guardian is the element of earth. From earth you learn the art of nurturing, the right use of your physical body

---

Let your body be comfortable, and take some deep breaths into your belly. Imagine yourself standing in the middle of your beautiful stone circle. Greet your symbols for the elements of air, fire, and water. Turning to face the final quarter in your circle, ask for guidance and energy from the element of earth to give you the grace and intent to nurture your deepest self.

Invite an earth guide to join you and support you in living from your core foundation. Be open to how that guide may appear. Your earth guide may be an animal, a person you know, or a stranger. It may be a quiet voice in your head, or a knowing in your body. Your guardian of earth may not come to you immediately, but later in a dream or while you are in the middle of your day. Earth may show its many forms to you. Pray for the power to nourish your being and create sacred boundaries.

When you feel complete, ask for a symbol to represent this new anchor, and place it in the final direction of your circle.

---

for your altar, pick an object to represent earth and place it in the final direction on the outside of the circle. You can represent earth with a rock, a statue of a person, or any object that pleases you. Set your intent to use all of the elements and their gifts to guide you to become deeply intimate with yourself, and manifest an inner container that reflects the strength of your center.

Be humble for you are made of earth.
Be noble for you are made of stars.

        Serbian Proverb

You must not for one instant give up
the effort to build new lives for
yourselves. Creativity means to push
open the heavy, groaning doorway to
life. This is not an easy struggle. Indeed,
it may be the most difficult
task in the world, for opening the door
to your own life is, in the end,
more difficult than opening the doors to
the mysteries of the universe.

        Daisaku Ikeda

the fifth element

When you consciously work with the elements of air, fire, water, and earth, you create a circle of support around your old belief system. Each gift of the elements is a tool to reclaim your own stuck energy and release what does not serve you. Now, for the second time, you build a structure, but this new structure is a temple constructed with awareness and joy.

You have everything you need within you to reclaim a sacred, possibility-filled life. It may take time, great patience, and much compassion. It is possible. The transformation leads you from living in a messy, cramped room to living in a huge, light-filled temple.

At any moment you can open your eyes to the truth. A magnificent, invisible temple surrounds the small room within yourself that you hide in. Looking from the inside out, you see yourself trapped in one tiny, gray room with a locked door. From the outside looking in, you see yourself curled in the corner of one room in a vast, many-roomed chamber of colors, textures, and space. And the door is open.

All the walls within your temple are alive. They breathe. They whisper to you, "You are huge. You are eternal. You are magnificent. You have gifts to share. Come out of your self-created room and claim your temple."

Your ears are tuned to the walls of your tiny room, which whisper, "This is all there is. Stay here, stay safe. You do not deserve to be bigger. You are already too big. Do not challenge the strength of these walls."

Nevertheless, you manage for seconds or days at a time to slip out and see the vastness around you. At these times the little room of your life dissolves and you are awed by the vision of eternity around you. Or you consciously step through the door and discover a new dream, beyond what you thought possible.

The transition between living in your familiar prison and living as big as the sky depends on a conscious use of the four elements. The elements and their gifts act as a foundation to pull your energy out of the unconscious rooms in your life. From this place, you can use these four anchors to weave a sacred base for a fifth point above your circle, pure essence. This magical place is the synergy of all four elements working together to create the fifth element, a direct connection to the infinite creative source of life.

When you live from the fifth element, you step into what you were always meant to become: a conscious temple, a direct reflection of spirit.

The first stage to stepping beyond your cramped rooms is to become conscious of your confinement. The second stage is building a new frame to surround your old structure. The third stage is pulling your energy from the old structure into your new, larger structure. And the fourth stage is realizing that there is not and never was any structure at all. This structureless place is the realm of the fifth element.

The structures we are talking about are created by your mind and energy. They are real and tangible and strong, and they are also illusions. Since they are created by the mind, they can be dissolved by the mind at a moment's notice. They are as real as you make them.

Once this new structure is in place, you will see your old structure with new eyes. The same emotions, fears, and disaster mind will be present, but instead of living them, you will witness them with love and perhaps even a smile on your face. Instead of using your mind, energy, emotions, and body against yourself, you will see all manifestations of fear and doubt as precious resources, as nuggets of potential energy that are simply trapped and waiting to be freed.

You are a vast, always centered, magical being. But your attention is hooked by the fears of the mind. The way out is to realize once and for all you are pure, unhindered energy.

You are a wild child of the universe, let loose in a magnificent playground to create whatever you dream possible. If you do not remember this with every fiber of your being by the time you read the end of this paragraph, I suggest you start by building a larger container for yourself, step by step, using the Four Elements of Change.

All humans have the ability to dance into the unknown and move beyond all structures in an instant. This could happen today, and it could happen the moment you die. This is the mystery. In the meantime, why not remodel your cramped quarters?

As you move into a larger conscious structure, your heart and soul expand to hold more love and energy. You move from limitations to possibilities.

This is not a one-way journey, but a path that will move back and forth between your old and new structures and infinity. There will be days or weeks or months at a time when you will forget the new structure and move back into your cramped room. It will seem as if nothing has changed, as if all the work you have done was in vain, as if you are a failure. But the new structure is there, waiting for you, supporting you.

There will be days or weeks or months at a time when you will live from your new structure, forgetting you ever lived any other way. You will feel balanced and present, open and nourished. Your life will unfold magically. Then one day you will find yourself unexpectedly slammed back into the middle of your old structure, or you will discover yourself slowly sliding without a foothold back into an old pattern. Can you keep your eyes open? If you can, you will learn and you will be able to bring energy and more awareness back into your new structure. If you plummet into complete forgetfulness, forgive yourself when you wake up again, and review what you have learned.

What I have seen is that as I have invested more and more of my energy in my new structure, the transitions between old and new are quicker. This felt a little strange at first. I would feel centered and balanced, get triggered by someone being upset with me at work or a fear of being abandoned, go into fear and judgment, but then pop out of it again quickly. Part of me would wonder why I was no longer upset.

I sometimes find myself staring at the place where an old structure used to be, wondering where it went, feeling awkward without it. There can be phantom limbs in our structure, places that are cleared out but that still hold a resonance, a memory. Eventually this, too, will dissolve. Do your best not to feed the old structure again, and instead allow yourself to be uncomfortable with the newness.

The move into the new structure completes the journey for some; for others it is only a beginning. You may choose to remodel your room, paint the walls and add some nice furnishings, and feel complete. Or you may look toward creating an entirely new structure, and moving into a bigger space. Perhaps you will even look beyond this structure, choose to release all structures and merge with the fifth element of infinity. Whether your focus is on a minor remodel or on a dissolution of all structures, the steps are the same. Perceive. Clean. Open. Nourish. Step by step, one moment at a time. From the new structure, you will better be able to live from your center.

Do not get overwhelmed by the task ahead of you. Keep your focus in the moment, on the current action. When you first begin to work with the gifts of the elements, start small. Pick one element at a time to practice. You can pick the element you feel most comfortable with, or the one you feel most uncomfortable with. Remember, the elements are not linear, but rather form a circle. The entry point to your healing lies anywhere within this circle.

For example, if you choose fire, the element of cleaning, give yourself small tasks to accomplish during the day. Set your intent and ask for guidance to help you learn about cleaning. Create touchstones to remind you of your focus: "Every time I light a candle or turn on a light, I will check in to see if there is anything within me I need to clean out." "This week I will light a candle and then clean some part of my house I've been putting off, to represent cleaning a part of myself I've been avoiding." "I am going to do one of the fire practices this week, a little each day."

As your energy shifts from one structure to another, a new world will open up. You will have the energy to create what you want. But do not try to skip any of the steps. It is better to be clear and systematic in the building of a new structure. Create a strong foundation with each of the elements. Really learn the art of perception. Practice the art of cleaning. Explore the art of opening. Manifest the art of nourishing in all aspects of your life.

In this way, you are in service to your true self, to your center. Your center lies within the very middle of your old structure, hidden deep in the foundation, buried under layers and layers of old beliefs and habits. It is pure and untouched, a jewel waiting to be brought into the light. Creating a new structure gives you the space to see the jewel within you, and the energy to unearth it.

As you reconfigure your old structure, the jewel within you shines more brightly. You begin to see the unique, precious being that you are. Comparison drops away as you value the perfection of who you are, right in this moment. You are the complex, multifaceted jewel, held by a structure of love. The structure of fear gets sandwiched between. You see without a doubt it does not have a chance of survival. Getting triggered or going into self-doubt and fear is no longer a disaster, but an exciting opportunity to reclaim more energy, to shine more brightly.

The goal is not outside of yourself, but within. What element can you use today to create more space for the brightness of your center? In this moment, how can you move into a larger structure, and give yourself room to grow?

Gradually your perceptions will begin to shift again. You will get flashes of another reality, an even larger vision. The center jewel of you, the unique, awesome, powerful light of you, is only a tiny star in a much bigger galaxy. Your nature is not to live in a limited structure, but to know yourself as part of the web of all possibilities. You become both a star in the temple of spirit, and the temple itself. You become the fifth element, pure non-duality and presence.

Right now, you are an infinite temple of life. You are a vast being. You are also a frightened child hiding in a corner, yearning for approval. Hold all of yourself, free and fearful, in the palms of your hands. In this way, you become a SpiritWeaver, weaving all of you, the sacred and mundane, into the fullness of your potential, clear and centered.

Resources

toltec center of creative intent / spiritweavers

The Toltec Center of Creative Intent in Berkeley, California, and our nationwide SpiritWeavers programs are dedicated to supporting individuals and communities in balancing mind, spirit, emotions, and body and becoming the artists of their lives. We offer:

Workshops and classes based on the wisdom of the Four Elements of Change, the Four Agreements, and other shamanic and healing traditions.

Power Journeys to Mexico, Peru, and Hawaii. These journeys are vital opportunities to step out of your old life, boost your energy, and reach greater depths of awareness.

SpiritWeavers Apprenticeship Circles. For those ready to go deeper on their spiritual journey, we offer a six-month intensive program based in shamanic wisdom. Join a community of people dedicated to living from their true center and integrity.

For a free e-newsletter or more information contact:
http://www.tolteccenter.org
info@tolteccenter.org • 510-649-0352

auDIOS BY HeatHeR asH

The Four Elements of Change Companion CD
Audio by Heather Ash
This CD contains guided meditations and practices from the book to enhance your journey toward center. Accompanied by music designed specifically for each of the elements.

Returning to Center: Meditation and Recapitulation CD
Audio by Heather Ash
Create your own daily practice of grounding and recapitulation. This CD includes a brief introduction and guided meditations for grounding and recapitulation. Includes an in-depth journey for clearing your energetic system.

Living an Impeccable Life
Audio by Heather Ash
A live lecture exploring what it means to be impeccable in the world. This CD gently guides the reader to move beyond using the internal judge to mark one's progress, and to cease striving to be perfect. From this viewpoint, impeccability stems from honesty and clear action.

All audios available at http://www.tolteccenter.org

recommended further reading

Abelar, Taisha. *The Sorcerers' Crossing.* Penguin, 1993.

Branton, Brad. *Radical Honesty: How to Transform Your Life.* Delta Publishing, 1994.

Beck, Renee, and Sydney Barabara Metrick. *The Art of Ritual: Creating and Performing Ceremonies for Growth and Change.* Celestial Arts, 2003.

Castaneda, Carlos. *Journey to Ixtlan.* Washington Square Press, 1991.

Castaneda, Carlos. *Power of Silence.* Washington Square Press, 1991.

Castaneda, Carlos. *The Wheel of Time: Shamans of Mexico and their Thoughts about Life, Death, and the Universe.* Washington Square Press, 2001.

Dibble, David. *The Four Agreements in the Workplace.* Emeritus, 2002.

Kingston, Karen. *Clear Your Clutter with Feng Shui.* Broadway Books, 1999.

Mares, Theun. *This Darned Elusive Happiness.* Lionheart Publishing, 1999.

Prechtel, Martin. *Secrets of the Talking Jaguar: Memoirs from the Living Heart of a Mayan Village.* Tarcher, 1999

Nelson, Mary Carroll. *Beyond Fear.* Council Oak Books, 1997.

Nelson, Mary Carroll. *Toltec Prophecies of don Miguel Ruiz.* Council Oak Books, 2003.

Noble, Vicki. *Shakti Woman: Feeling Our Fire, Healing Our World.* Harper Collins, 1991.

Rosenburg, Marshall B. *Non-Violent Communication: A Language of Compassion.* Puddle Dancer Press, 1989.

Ruiz, Miguel. *The Four Agreements.* Amber-Allen Publishing, 1997.

Ruiz, Miguel. *The Mastery of Love.* Amber-Allen Publishing, 1999.

Sanchez, Victor, Robert Nelson, translator. *Teachings of Don Carlos: Practical Applications of the Works of Carlos Castaneda.* Bear & Co., 1995.

Starhawk. *The Spiral Dance.* Harper Collins, 1999.

Stone, Hal and Sidra. *Embracing Our Selves.* New World Library, 1989.

Tunneshende, Marilyn. *Don Juan and the Art of Sexual Energy.* Bear & Co. 2001.

Vigil, Bernadette. *Mastery of Awareness.* Bear & Co., 2002.

Weinstein, Marion. *Positive Magic.* New Page, 2002.

Many of the above books, and CD's of live lectures
with Heather Ash, are available at
http://www.tolteccenter.org

Toltec Center of Creative Intent
PO Box 12216
Berkeley, CA 94712
510-649-0352

HeatHeR asH weaves the most powerful practices from a variety of shamanic traditions to support each individual in the manifestation of his or her highest potential. She is the founder of the Toltec Center of Creative Intent in Berkeley, CA, and the creator of nationwide SpiritWeavers programs, designed to support spirit-based community. Heather Ash studied and taught extensively with don Miguel Ruiz, author of *The Four Agreements*, and is a Mentor in his Eagle Knight lineage.

COUNCIL oak BOOKS since 1984 has published books from all over the world, books that, like this one, cross cultural lines to bring together ancient traditions in new ways. Drawing from history, we publish for the future, presenting books that point the way to a richer life and a better world.